John Winthrop, Oliver Cromwell, and the Land of Promise

John Winthrop, Oliver Cromwell, and

the Land of Promise

Marc Aronson

CLARION BOOKS · NEW YORK

Clarion Books
a Houghton Mifflin Company imprint
215 Park Avenue South, New York, NY 10003
Copyright © 2004 by Marc Aronson

The text was set in 12-point Fournier.
Book design by Trish Parcell Watts.
Maps on pages 47 and 107 by Kayley LeFaiver.

For information about permission to reproduce selections from this book, write to
Permissions, Houghton Mifflin Company,
215 Park Avenue South, New York, NY 10003.

www.houghtonmifflinbooks.com

Printed in the U. S. A.

Library of Congress Cataloging-in-Publication Data

Aronson, Marc.
John Winthrop, Oliver Cromwell, and the Land of Promise / by Marc Aronson.
p. cm.
Summary: Looks at how the lives of John Winthrop, governor of Massachusetts, and Oliver
Cromwell, Lord Protector of the Puritan Commonwealth in England, were intertwined at a
time of conflict between church and state and between Native and European Americans.
Includes bibliographical references (p.   ) and index.
ISBN 0-618-18177-6
1. Winthrop, John, 1588–1649—Juvenile literature. 2. Puritans—Massachusetts—
Biography—Juvenile literature. 3. Governors—Massachusetts—Biography—Juvenile lit-
erature. 4. Massachusetts—History—Colonial period, ca. 1600–1775—Juvenile literature.
5. Puritans—History—17th century—Juvenile literature. 6. Cromwell, Oliver,
1599–1658—Juvenile literature. 7. Heads of state—Great Britain—Biography—Juvenile
literature. 8. Generals—Great Britain—Biography—Juvenile literature. 9. Great Britain—
History—Puritan Revolution, 1642–1660—Juvenile literature. 10. Great Britain—
History—Early Stuarts, 1603–1649—Juvenile literature. [1. Winthrop, John, 1588–1649. 2.
Governors. 3. Puritans. 4. Massachusetts—History—Colonial period, ca. 1600–1775. 5.
Cromwell, Oliver, 1599–1658. 6. Heads of state. 7. Generals. 8. Great Britain—History—
Puritan Revolution, 1642–1660. 9. Great Britain—History—Early Stuarts, 1603–1649.] I.
Title.
F67.W79A76 2004   974.4'02—dc22   2003016418

VB 10 9 8 7 6 5 4 3 2 1

To my many, many relatives in Israel who, daily, experience another version of the modern holy war for the Promised Land.
I hope that this history of parallel issues in Britain and America may offer some insight and perspective for your own daunting challenges.

To the fathers and sons in The Real Thing, my nonfiction reading group. I always learn more from you than I give you.

And, always, to Sasha. Someday I will write a book not only dedicated to you but for you to read.

CONTENTS

ACKNOWLEDGMENTS

Writing a book such as this, which seeks to combine so many threads, incurs many debts of gratitude. My thanks to Virginia Buckley for her detailed and engaged editing; to Renée Cafiero for indefatigable vigilance; to Joann Hill for sharing my vision of the book; to André Carus for his bibliographic suggestions and general advice on the English Civil War; to Robert Mitchell and Patrick Hargan for sharing their many Indigo Jones with me; and to Dr. Francis Bremer, editor of the Winthrop papers, for a thorough and helpful reading that saved me from errors and introduced me to two recent books that changed my views on key events. Unfortunately, I received his own definitive and readable new biography, *John Winthrop: America's Forgotten Founding Father* (Oxford University Press, 2003), too late to use as a major resource, but in its dual focus on England and America, its wonderful level of detail, and its approachable style, it is the ideal book for any motivated student or teacher who is inspired to learn more about Winthrop. Of course, in spite of having received excellent academic advice, any remaining gaffes in this work are entirely of my own making. I am grateful, also, to Dr. Alberto Goldwaser for his many challenging questions; and especially to my wife, Marina Budhos, for creating the home, the family life, and the ever-fascinating creative and intellectual atmosphere that made this book possible.

WHY THIS BOOK

A militant religious leader urges his followers to martyr themselves for the holy cause. Another demands that moderate leaders be destroyed, for they are the enemies of God. A third leads armed bands to destroy images and sculptures that he claims offend God. Seeing that the peace and security of his nation are threatened by these dangerous extremists, a ruler who would really rather spend his time with his devoted wife and his clever friends decides he must imprison the fanatics; when that fails, he declares war on them. This may sound like a summary of contemporary news bulletins, but it is not—it is a description of events in the seventeenth century in England and New England as they might have been described by a sensationalist headline writer.

Today it is America and the West that are the targets of extremists, who use the language of Islam to preach holy war. In the seventeenth century, though, Protestant religious zealots became leaders in both England and New England. Ironically, they and not their more tempered opponents were directly responsible for creating the West we know today. We are the heirs of the radicals, not of the established government.

Inspired by their faith, Oliver Cromwell in England and John Winthrop in New England attempted to create Heaven on Earth. They sincerely believed that they were at the end of time; that they were fighting the first battles of the final war that would bring the return of Jesus. This passionate belief allowed Cromwell to turn untrained men into the best cavalry in England, perhaps in all Europe. It gave Winthrop the strength to establish a strong colony on New England's rocky soil. And when their dreams of perfect living faded, Cromwell, Winthrop, and their fellow believers began to realize that new principles would be necessary for human beings to live together well—ideas such as religious tolerance, political democracy, and greater social equality.

This book is the story of a time, almost four centuries ago, hauntingly similar to our own era—with some crucial role reversals. It is about the hope that America was destined to be the home of a utopia in which human beings would live ideal lives, that this was the Promised Land in which the second coming of Jesus would take place. That dream is still alive today. But this book is also about the growing realization that human societies are always run by imperfect people. The raucous disputes of a political democracy, not the fervent and carefully monitored prayers of the faithful, offer the best chance for good government. It is precisely that shift from the ideal to the practical that most offends modern extremists, who, like our own ancestors, will settle for nothing less than perfection—even if they have to kill to achieve it.

As you will see, the ideas we associate with being American were as much a result of people and events in the England of the 1630s and 1640s as of anything that happened in Massachusetts, Philadelphia, and Virginia 130 years later. American history *is* world history. In my first book on the colonial era, *Sir Walter Ralegh and the Quest for El Dorado* (Clarion, 2000), I tried to show what the dream, the fantasy of America, meant to the English. As the New World became less a site for the dreams of conquistadors, explorers, and mystics, and more a place of settlement for people waiting for the second coming of Jesus, or simply wanting to live better lives, it was no less bound up with English history.

This book describes events in both England and New England because the seventeenth-century people I describe could not have imagined them as separate. Only by recovering these links across the Atlantic can we make sense of our global past, or our global present.

Cast of Characters

England, Scotland, Ireland

Elizabethans

Elizabeth I
Sir Walter Ralegh
Mary Stuart, Queen of Scots
Thomas Hariot

The King, His Allies, Family, and Supporters (Cavaliers)

Charles I
James I, his father
Henrietta Maria, his wife
Henry, his brother, died in 1612
William Laud, Archbishop of Canterbury in the Church of England
Thomas Wentworth, Earl of Strafford
Prince Rupert, Royal General of the Horse
Sir John Suckling, poet, soldier
James Butler, Duke of Ormonde
William Cavendish, Earl of Newcastle
James Graham, Marquis of Montrose
Sir Marmaduke Langdale

Artists in or Allied with the Court

Inigo Jones, set designer, architect
Thomas Carew, poet, playwright
Richard Lovelace, poet
Edmund Waller, poet

OPPONENTS OF THE KING (Independents, Puritans, Roundheads)

Advocates
William Prynne
Stephen Marshall
Parliamentarians
John Hampden
John Pym
Oliver St. John
Denzil Holles
Soldiers
Oliver Cromwell, Lord Protector
Richard Cromwell, son of Oliver
Robert Devereux, Earl of Essex
Major General Philip Skippon
Edward Montagu, Earl of Manchester
Thomas Fairfax
Henry Ireton, son-in-law of Cromwell, also active in Parliament
James Pitson
George Joyce

OTHER OPPONENTS

Scots Presbyterians
John Knox
Alexander Leslie
Thomas Pride
Visionaries
Robert Crab, the mad hatter
Gerrard Winstanley, leader of the Diggers
George Fox, founder of the Religious Society of Friends (Quakers)
Levellers—Political and Social Radicals
Colonel Thomas Rainborough
John Lilburne
John Wildman
Edward Sexby
Katherine Chidley

Poets
Andrew Marvell
John Milton

NEW WORLD

PURITANS, THEIR FAMILIES, ALLIES, SUPPORTERS

John Winthrop (married to Margaret)
John Cotton
Thomas Dudley
Thomas Shepard
Increase Nowell

SOLDIERS

John Mason
John Underhill

CRITICS OF PURITAN GOVERNMENT AND RELIGIOUS PRACTICE

Roger Williams (married to Mary)
Anne Hutchinson (married to William, a wealthy merchant)
Henry Vane Jr.
John Wheelwright

NON-PURITAN LEADERS

William Bradford (Plymouth Plantation)

NATIVE PEOPLES

Narragansett
Pequot
Mohegan
Niantic

PROLOGUE

WHO RULES ENGLAND?

A ROYAL SPECTACLE

Charles I is seated on a magnificent throne of gold decorated with palm trees and statues of ancient heroes. England's king and his grandest nobles are dressed in blue embroidered with silver, their silver caps adorned with gold scrolls and white feathers. Slowly a multicolored cloud descends from the heavens, carrying his queen, Henrietta Maria, and her ladies dressed in fine silks of red and silver, with plumed helmets and carrying swords. As befits a goddess, rays of light stream from behind Henrietta Maria's head. The appreciative court breaks into a song of praise for the glorious king and his ravishing queen:

> *All that are harsh, all that are rude,*
> *Are by your harmony subdued.*

With this triumphal ending to a royal spectacle, King Charles in 1640 celebrated and demonstrated his glory, his goodness, and his power. It was the last such event he ever staged.

Top: *The border of a set for the royal masque called* The Temple of Love. *This set was designed by Inigo Jones, who was also an important architect. Jones followed the breakthroughs in theater and painting in Italy and introduced to England what we would now call "special effects" and tricks of design that dazzled audiences. One of these innovations was to have a proscenium, or border, around the stage. He then used his knowledge of perspective to fool the eye and make the stage seem to extend endlessly into the distance.* Left: *Sketch by Inigo Jones for a masquer's costume.*

ANTICHRIST

*. . . it is the last time: and as ye have heard that antichrist shall come,
even now are there many antichrists; whereby we know that it is the last
time.*

1 JOHN 2:18

Even as Charles dazzled the high nobility, throughout England men and
women, rich and poor, drew their inspiration from a very different source:
the holy Bible. Many of these readers believed that the New Testament's
Book of Revelation held the key to understanding their tumultuous times.
Today scholars believe it was originally meant to inspire, give courage to,
and strengthen the resolve of very early Christian communities. Written in
cryptic and symbolic language, Revelation is a vivid sequence of visions
and prophecies that describe the ultimate battle between good and evil that
has already begun.

Revelation is terrifying both because it predicts that death and destruction are coming soon and because of the sharp lines it draws between the
saved and the damned. But it is also reassuring, for no matter how much a
person may be suffering now, in the end Jesus and the saved will triumph
over Satan, over the scarlet woman—the Whore of Babylon riding on the
seven-headed monster—over the massed forces of those marked with 666,
the number of the beast. The saved will include 12,000 members of each of
the twelve tribes of Israel, 144,000 souls in all. After Satan is cast away, the
chosen will rule on Earth for a thousand peaceful years, before the battle of
Armageddon—the very last stand of evil, which will lead to the final reign
of Jesus.

Many English Protestants in the seventeenth century did not interpret

In this anonymous 1643 drawing, the Pope is seated on a seven-headed beast. The nightmarish image makes it clear that he, the Catholic Church, and the Church of England are all evils foretold in the Bible, and that the battles of the final days have begun

(CATALOGUE OF PERSONAL AND POLITICAL SATIRES, THE BRITISH MUSEUM, 378.)

the Book of Revelation as a commentary on the early days of Christianity; instead, they believed it held coded messages, and clear prophecies, for their own time. What could the seven-headed beast be but Rome, the city of seven hills? Roman Catholicism must be the false prophecy, the religion of the Antichrist, the enemy of Jesus who Revelation predicted would appear to delude people in the final days. Influential writers such as John Foxe and Joseph Mede explained that Catholics, the Pope, even lordly English kings who were too friendly to Catholics, were the forces of the Antichrist. There was no longer any time to wait. Everyone would be called to choose the side of final good or absolute evil.

The Bible itself seemed to say that no matter how lavish the court of the king, it was as nothing, and a time of reckoning was coming, coming very soon.

THE PROPHET

Robert Crab was said to be "mad as a hatter"; in fact, the phrase itself was invented to describe him. Born in 1621, Crab was a hat maker, and he read his New Testament very carefully. When he meditated on Jesus' instruction "If thou wilt be perfect, go and sell that thou hast, and give to the poor" (Matthew 19:21), he sold everything he possessed or gave it away. That was but the first step: He limited his diet to vegetables and water, later to just leaves and grass; he made his own clothes, took a vow of celibacy, renounced war, and preached. "Property," Crab declared, moved the "murderer to kill, and the thief to steal."

Crab died in 1680, having made but one known convert. While his legacy was merely the example of how "mad" a person could become, Crab was an extreme instance of a very dangerous tendency. If people read their Bible as criticizing not only the king but all manner of Earthly power and luxury, how could England be governed?

In the middle years of the seventeenth century, Charles and his luxurious court, devoted students of the Bible inspired to risk all for their faith, and social prophets preaching radical democracy collided and produced the ideas that would later give birth to the United States. This is the story of that clash.

THE GODLY

CHAPTER ONE

THE BRITISH HEAVEN

"NOTORIOUS WHORES"

The Queen liked to dance.

Charles I was the king of England. He succeeded his father, James I, who had journeyed from Scotland to take the crown when a dying Queen Elizabeth I named him as her heir. Unlike so many monarchs throughout history, Charles truly loved his wife, the French-born Henrietta Maria, who was both his heart's desire and his best friend. Like her relatives, his fellow rulers in Europe, Charles enjoyed beautiful things. He understood painting so well that great artists admired his judgment, and he in turn commissioned portraits and ceiling paintings from Europe's best painters. The king ordered lavish performances to be staged just for his family and the high nobles of the court. Called masques, these spectacles were more than plays, for they included music and songs. At a special moment the costumed players would leave the sets and come to dance with the audience. And the queen, the Catholic queen of Protestant England, liked to dance. Unmarried women who danced in the masques wore costumes that exposed their breasts for all to see. But even more modestly dressed wives and mothers were inviting men to look at them, at their bodies. This infuriated those who believed women should be demure, silent, and invisible.

In 1634 a devout Protestant lawyer named William Prynne published a condemnation of plays and the theater called *Histrio-Mastix* and created a scandal. The most inflammatory line in it appeared, of all places, in the index. Under the heading for "woman actors" Prynne added the words "notorious whores." Everyone knew that Prynne was calling the nimble-footed queen who acted in plays a fallen woman who displayed her body to men.

Charles and Henrietta Maria, as painted by Daniel Mytens. The king and queen were a rare example of a royal couple who truly loved each other.   (ROYAL COLLECTION COPYRIGHT 2003, HER MAJESTY QUEEN ELIZABETH II)

Prynne was arrested. His fellow lawyers responded by staging a special masque of their own for their king—hoping it might at least spare them from his wrath. Charles did enjoy the masque, but Prynne was tried and convicted. His punishments included a large fine, losing his license to practice law, a sentence of life imprisonment in the Tower of London, and having his ears cut off. What greater contrast could there be: a bejeweled court laughing and twirling at Charles's magnificent entertainments, and a bloodied William Prynne dragged off to the Tower for insulting the queen? But who was right—the king furiously defending his wife, or the religious radical, adamantly condemning his queen?

Prynne was an extremist who believed that kings who violated God's laws should be overthrown. His fury at the idea of a woman drawing the attention of men to her body is shared today by religious fundamentalists who object to women appearing in public unless they are completely covered. He was such a committed anti-Semite that he opposed even his own Protestant allies when they wanted to ease restrictions against Jews. Today we fight wars against such religious extremists when they attack us, and we support governments that jail them. How different is that from Charles, who can be seen as simply trying to control a dangerous, and insulting, fanatic?

Yet Prynne was not merely a religious radical bent on imposing his extreme views on England. He believed that each man had an obligation higher than his duty to the crown, and that was duty to his conscience and to the law. No one, not even the king himself, was above the laws of God, as set forth in the New Testament, and the laws of men, as passed down through English history. Each Englishman was a kind of mini-king ruling himself and his family, and the nation needed all these devout and thoughtful men to speak out. This was precisely the view Charles rejected. He believed that the

In this satirical image, William Laud (the Archbishop of Canterbury) is served various delicacies, including William Prynne's ears. Between 1640 and 1662 the successive English governments were not able or willing to control the press. As a result, within that period a much wider range of opinions and political satires appeared in print than before or after. When Charles was more firmly in control, an image like this would have been suppressed.

(COURTESY OF ASHMOLEAN MUSEUM, OXFORD, AND UK/BRIDGEMAN ART LIBRARY)

country was best run from the top down, with a wise, virtuous king direct-ing humble and obedient men and women, ruling by divine right. Bottom up or top down, this was the central issue England had to decide.

THE WEALTHIEST COMMONER IN ALL ENGLAND

Passionately held religious views were not the only reason people resisted Charles's plan for top-down rule. There was also the tricky matter of law. Was the king God's representative on Earth, and so above the petty regula-tions that bound lesser men? Or was the king the ruler because he upheld the rules that tied all England together? In families a parent often says something is the rule "because I say so." Charles thought he should have the same authority over his nation, and he viewed any who disagreed with him as disobedient children who needed to be punished. John Hampden disagreed.

Even though he was not of noble birth, Hampden might easily have been invited to join in the audience at Charles's court. He was said to be the richest man in England—who was not an earl, or duke, or baron, or prince. His family could point to an unbroken sequence of honorable ancestors stretching back even before 1066, when the Normans conquered England. Like William Prynne, John Hampden was a devout Protestant, but he was not the same kind of fire-breathing zealot. Plays didn't bother him; royal arrogance did. Hampden got himself elected to Parliament in order to challenge the king.

Like his father, Charles did not want to have to beg, wheedle, and negotiate with Parliament for money. That was demeaning. It implied that common men had a right to judge, to question, a king. He actually did want to do well by his country, and in turn he thought his subjects should give their support and, if necessary, their money to enable him to do whatever he believed was right.

John Hampden did not think the king should be able to receive any money unless it was authorized by Parliament. It was not that he was unwilling to pay taxes; rather, he was unwilling to pay taxes that he and the other members of Parliament had not agreed to pay. As Americans would put it a century and a half later, "no taxation without representation."

Charles could not be bothered to haggle with men like Hampden. In 1629 he closed Parliament, told the members to go home, and tried to rule without them. Instead of bargaining with legislators, Charles found a clever way to use an old tax in a new way. "Ship money" was a fee that taxpayers who lived near the coast paid for the upkeep of the navy that protected them. In 1635 Charles decided that everyone should have to contribute, no matter where they lived. The following year he came back for more money, and then again in 1637. Hampden protested. He claimed that there was no real need for the tax, and that the king could not collect it without the approval of Parliament. The king asked the court to decide the matter. A panel of twelve judges discussed the issue for twelve days before finally ruling 7–5 that the tax was legal because the king imposed it. He could bend, break, or change the law however he wanted. "Rex is lex," the king is the law, they said.

Though the king won the case, the narrow majority and even the suit itself showed that many strong-willed Englishmen believed just the opposite: The king rules only when he obeys the law. One set of English people was challenging the king for such offenses to faith as having a wife who was Catholic and liked to act in plays. Another insisted that not even his royal blood, his crown and scepter, made him different from the most common beggar. All of England, they argued, must uphold the same laws.

Now it was Charles who disagreed. To him a king was the instrument of God. To challenge a king was to violate God's plan for the world. His critics were like petty criminals sullying something beautiful they could not understand. As he savored the lavish creations of the most gifted artists in Europe, and gazed on the elegant clothing of the nobles gathered to honor him in his court, Charles viewed his critics as vile, base, beneath contempt.

According to some accounts, when Hampden lost the case, he also began to lose faith in England. And in 1638 he may have prepared to leave for America. The New World seemed like a refuge to him. To the king it was a kind of garbage dump.

"No Bishop, No King"

Perhaps the most brilliant of the masques staged for Charles was titled *Coelum Britannicum, The British Heaven*. One dazzling special effect the talented architect and designer Inigo Jones created for the show was a giant globe that was held in place by Atlas, the ancient Greek god.

The globe was lit from behind, revealing the constellations in the sky. But the stories of the Greek gods and heroes who gave their names to those starry figures were tales of seduction and intrigue, jealousy and betrayal. Faced with the magnificent example of the faithful King Charles and his devoted wife, the old constellations began to blink out, one by one. Scorpions, fish, goats, and the rest of the creatures of the zodiac were banished from the sky. Actors and costumed nobles performed a backward dance, capturing the scuttling motion of Cancer, the deposed heavenly crab.

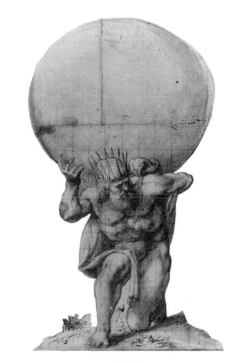

Top: *Atlas holding a globe, as designed by Inigo Jones for* The British Heaven, *awed the audience when the sphere glowed with the constellations from the sky. Jones's stage tricks were as impressive to his audience as the most sophisticated computer-enhanced movie animations are to us today.* Center and Bottom: *Toward the end of* The British Heaven *a cloud appeared and then parted to reveal the spirit of poetry.*

Above: *Set for the opening scene of* The British Heaven, *as designed by Inigo Jones. The ruins framed the stage and suggested lost ancient civilizations, now replaced by the glory of King Charles.* Right: *Momus, the spirit of satire, one of the main characters in* The British Heaven.

What would become of these vile creatures? One of the players suggested that it would be a very good idea if they all gathered together in a tall ship and sailed off to New England. The god Mercury agreed that the New England radicals

> *. . . cannot breath this pure and temperate air*
> *Where Virtue lives, but will with hasty flight,*
> *'Mongst fogs and vapors, seek unsound abodes.*

He then commanded the remaining stars to join the "foul remainders of that viperous brood" in their exile.

Seen from the vantage of Charles and his court, the Puritan settlers of New England, who figure so importantly in American history, were unpleasant, dangerous extremists who threatened the harmony of their homeland. Purging them from England was like expelling a disease. It is not hard to see why he felt that way.

Every effort the king made to put in place efficient leaders to bring order to the churches of England and Scotland; every falling-down, decrepit church he repaired and made beautiful; every priest he praised for reassuring people that they were not damned before birth by a cold, distant God; every step he took to make life easier for Catholics—all these inspired condemnation, suspicion, and rage from the religious radicals. If these malcontents were eager to cross the ocean to establish their own brand of Heaven on Earth in the wild and dangerous lands of the New World, good riddance!

Charles viewed religion exactly the same way he did government: They both needed a moral, devout leader who set a good example. His powerful and learned bishops, cloaked in their beautiful garments, conducted services in churches where incense perfumed the air and colored light danced through lush stained-glass windows. The magnificence of the churches gave every worshiper a sense of being in a holy place. The Book of Common Prayer, like the King James translation of the Bible that his father had commissioned, made religion an experience all could share in, as long as they listened to their leaders. Those who criticized this harmonious world of approved texts, wise bishops, and humble congregations were as traitorous and disruptive as the argumentative lawyers and rebellious Parliamentarians. As James had put it, "no bishop, no king."

The religious extremists who wanted to eliminate bishops and elaborate rituals were similar to the angry Parliamentarians who challenged the authority of the king, and were in fact often the same people. God was a fierce presence that commanded each and every one of them to relentlessly scour his conscience. To accept lulling services, to ignore debauchery in the royal court, was as bad as paying an illegal tax or bowing to a false god.

The word "Puritan" was a negative term used by the enemies of believers who called themselves the godly. The godly saw Charles and his archbishop, William Laud, slowly but surely undermining the true Protestant faith. Not only were these leaders allowing women to dance, but they encouraged people to violate the holy Sabbath by engaging in sports and playing games. They even revived pagan rituals such as dancing around the Maypole. The Puritans and their allies believed that Protestantism all around the world was in danger, and that England, the last best hope of God's truth, was being corrupted by Catholics like Henrietta Maria, and by Catholic sympathizers such as Archbishop Laud. The pure fire of Protestant faith was in danger of being snuffed out. No wonder that in the 1630s between 15,000 and 20,000 English people, perhaps half of whom were Puritans, undertook the dangerous journey across the ocean in a Great Migration to New England.

THE PUZZLE OF THE THREE KINGDOMS

Charles was able to expunge some of his malcontents by letting them escape to America. But even that outlet could not bring peace and calm to his land. Charles journeyed to Edinburgh, Scotland, in 1633 for the first time since he was three years old. The two kingdoms were drawing closer, for his father had ruled as king of both England and Scotland, and Charles arrived for his own coronation as the ruler of the northern kingdom. But the land Charles came to visit was not easily ruled. Scotland itself was just reaching the end of a long struggle between highlanders and lowlanders.

The dire threats to England exposed. Many Protestants and supporters of Parliament believed that Catholics in and outside the country were plotting against them. (THE FOTOMAS INDEX)

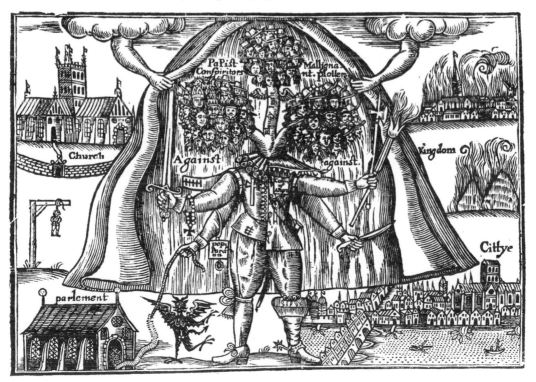

The windswept islands, the high mountains, and the steep gorges of Scotland were ruled by clans with names such as Macdonald and Macleod, Mackay and Ross, Campbell and Maclean. The word "clan" comes from the Gaelic *clann*, or "children," and each group looked to its leader, or laird, as a kind of father of the tribe. These were the bearded Scottish men of legend, who wore kilts and fought fierce and endless battles with each other and against the lowlanders. The tartan plaids that people wear to this day are like the colors of modern gangs; what you wore showed who you were. The highlanders tended to be Catholics.

Scots who lived closer to England in the lowlands were in general more influenced by English ideas. Over the centuries the lowlanders gradually wrested control of all Scotland from the ancient clans. But at any moment a laird could lead his people into a new alliance that would disrupt the balance of the kingdom. An even more ominous divide had developed in recent years.

In order to defeat her cousin Mary, Queen of Scots, Queen Elizabeth had made an alliance with the most fervent Scottish Protestants, led by the eloquent and uncompromising priest John Knox. This meant that people of the same temper as the English Puritans were the dominant religious force just across the northern border.

The Scottish church established by Knox and his supporters was stark and bare in its aspect, ferociously judgmental in its opinions. Christmas and Easter celebrations were banned. No music was allowed except for the human voice, and churches had no decorations. Despite his alliance with Elizabeth, Knox did not mince words about his distaste for females holding any kind of power. He wrote a pamphlet condemning "The Monstrous Regiment of Women," in which he announced that any woman ruler was "repugnant to nature" and insulting to God. This was the land Charles, the love-struck husband of a bejeweled Catholic wife, had come to rule.

The coronation of Charles as King of Scotland took place in the church of St. Giles, where flickering candles glinted off the rich robes of bishops. Charles was determined to bring the severe Scots into line with the more moderate brand of faith he and Archbishop Laud were enforcing in England. How could he possibly do that? One answer seemed almost too perfect, for it would solve two problems at once. If poor Protestant Scots were given land in Catholic Ireland, Charles would spread out the zealots, making Scotland a wealthier, happier place while extending his control of the Ireland that the English had been struggling to rule since the days of Queen Elizabeth and Sir Walter Ralegh.

Colonies, at the time, were often called "plantations," since new people were trying to take root in foreign soil. Ralegh had tried, and failed, to "plant" his Devonshire countrymen in Ireland. Undaunted, first James and then Charles encouraged over 100,000 Scots, Welsh, and English subjects to take over Irish land. Compared to this massive effort at colonization, the English presence in New England hardly mattered. What of those already on the island? As in Ralegh's day, the Irish—but this time also earlier English settlers—were evicted from their land. This effort was concentrated in the county of Ulster, which became the borderland between a still largely Catholic Ireland and a Scots-Irish Protestant settlement. It is precisely there that battles between faiths have been fought right down to the present day.

The blending of Scots and Irish traditions did, though, have an effect on American history. During the 1700s as many as half of the Ulster Scots moved on to America. The Scots-Irish immigrants who settled many frontier regions from the Appalachians to the west, and contributed so much to

American folklore, music, and culture, are their direct descendants. The lessons they learned in Scotland and Ireland were to never trust the English and to fight fiercely to be independent. One more effort of Charles's to pacify his homelands bred a new set of "infectious persons" to populate his foggy colony overseas.

Here then was the puzzle of the three kingdoms: The more the radical Protestants in Scotland resisted Charles, the more tempted he was to use Catholic troops from Ireland against them. Doing that would infuriate English Protestants, who already feared and resented the creeping Catholicism being enforced by Archbishop Laud, and might undermine the new Protestant plantations in Ireland. On the other hand, if Catholics rose up in Ireland, or if, just as Ralegh and Elizabeth had feared, the Catholic powers of Spain and France used Ireland as a beachhead to attack England, Charles would have to ally himself with the Protestant radicals he detested. And even if he were willing to take any of these risks, arming soldiers would mean paying for them, which only Parliament could authorize. Calling Parliament was the one thing Charles did not want to do.

In spectacles staged for his court, such as *The British Heaven*, Charles reigned supreme. But outside the doors of his palace, each land he ruled balanced precariously between radical Protestants willing to take any risk for their faith and frustrated Catholics tempted to ally with England's enemies. Should the bitter rivalries in any of these volatile places get even slightly out of hand, all three kingdoms could collapse into chaos. And no stage tricks could save Charles or those he ruled from that British Hell.

CHAPTER TWO

JOHN WINTHROP

MANY PLEASURES, ONE TRUE JOY

Why did an extreme form of Protestantism appeal to so many of the English? Why did it drive them across the Atlantic and inspire them to challenge their king, at the cost of their homes, their safety, sometimes their lives? The life and story of John Winthrop provides one good answer.

The godly were determined to awaken everyone to God, and they did so with both bold passion and clear logic. Their ministers were the ancestors of modern-day revivalists. A great preacher such as John Rogers would make the pulpit "roar," drawing crowds of more than a thousand people. His words would crash like thunder and flash like lightning. But these orators did not merely rely on grand emotional displays. The Puritans developed what they termed a "plain style" of clear, logical address. To many listeners they seemed more devoted to God's word than did ministers who would go along with whatever the king wanted to hear. The pure and plain gospel, with its terrifying warnings about the state of one's soul, seemed to many a truth they had always half known and now must face.

The gospel made converts in another way, too. As long as England had been a Catholic country, it had had to obey the Pope's commandment that the Bible must be written in Latin. This rule insured that only the most educated people could read the Bible. Protestants believed that the Bible by itself could instruct people, which is why King James sponsored a new edition that made it available in English. By 1640 over a million Bibles had been printed in England. More and more individuals could read, and now, for the very first time in history, they had direct access to the word of God.

Since God had finally released his word to the people, it stood to reason that more revelations would soon follow. Many of the new Bible readers attempted to puzzle out the Good Book's hidden meanings. At home, poring over the sacred text, each person tried to match the day's events to the prophecies and revelations they read. The Bible provided a route map, an explanation, for daily life. A convincing preacher, then, not only made a sinner look into his or her soul, he also mapped out the few remaining days of human history and showed how they had been predicted in the Bible.

One man who found this kind of soul-stirring, truth-telling sermon convincing was young John Winthrop. John had been born in the great Armada year of 1588. Defeating Catholics held a very personal meaning for the Winthrop clan. John's grandfather had purchased the family estate of Groton Manor when Henry VIII confiscated and sold off the lands held by monasteries. If Catholics returned to power in England, there was a chance that the Winthrops would lose their home. During John's childhood, though, Groton was a wonderful place to be. As one of the great historians of the Puritans describes it, the land was "gently rolling country, checkered with dark wood lots and bright fields of wheat, rye, peas, barley, hops, with here and there a shallow pond, stocked with fat carp." The family's only son, John liked walking in the fields, hunting, savoring the bounty of the estate he was born to manage. But he was nagged by a sense that he enjoyed all these good things too much.

We do not know the precise moment when Winthrop changed from being a regular but firm Protestant to becoming one of the godly. But the spiritual journey he recorded is one of the clearest accounts of what it meant to be so intoxicated with God.

Winthrop began keeping a diary at age nineteen, and his writing has the obsessive intensity of any religious seeker's private record. He worried about his love of hunting, which bothered others, risked a stiff fine, and took up too much of his time. His resolve to give up shooting was made eas-

What remains of Groton Manor is now called Groton Place. A new front was added after John Winthrop's time, but the structure of the building is the same as it was in his day.

(COURTESY OF REFERENCE LIBRARY, BOROUGH OF BURY ST. EDMUNDS)

ier by the fact that he hardly ever hit anything. But this itself was a sign—if he could not do something well, it was an indulgence to continue. Winthrop was bothered by how much he enjoyed eating, and set limits to what he'd take in each meal. He didn't like himself when he played cards, so he swore not to and made sure his servants didn't either. All these small resolutions led up to a twelve-point plan to do his work well, teach his family in the ways of the Lord, and observe the Sabbath.

There was just one problem with Winthrop's endless resolutions and good intentions: He knew he was doomed to fail. In fact, all he gained was to feel worse when he not only indulged in his old weaknesses but broke his new vows. The events of Winthrop's life intervened to show him that this cycle of weak effort was not getting him anywhere.

John seems to have enjoyed having sex, which was just as it should have been for a Puritan. The challenge for Puritans was to partake of all of the goodness God brought to the world, including sexual relations between husband and wife, but never to become too attached to any of those pleasures. They could not renounce temptation and live in protected communities, as Catholic priests and nuns did. They must savor everything God created for enjoyment, for to reject those pleasures was to turn away from the bounty God provided for humans. And yet, at the very same time, they must always remember that nothing physical mattered at all.

As the poet Andrew Marvell put it, the soul is

> . . . *hung up, as 'twere, in chains*
> *Of nerves, and arteries, and veins.*
> *Tortured, besides each other part,*
> *In a vain head, and double heart.*

A Puritan had to be "in" the world of temptation and pleasure, but not "of" it, not ruled by those passions.

Winthrop married at seventeen, eleven years younger than the average at the time, and his first child was born ten months later. Winthrop's first wife died after ten years, in 1615. In an age when diseases were rampant and doctors had no cures, the early death of a spouse was not unusual, and widows or widowers were expected to quickly remarry. Within six months John had met and married his second wife, Thomasine Clopton. But she died just a year later after a difficult childbirth. Thomasine was a devout woman, and as she was dying, she used her own example to urge her family to think of God. Her death, and her piety, challenged Winthrop. "I cannot serve two masters," he realized. If he remained too attached to the world, he could not love God.

John Winthrop was now entering into the heart of a Puritan's most difficult and precious experience. He understood that he must be *in* the world yet not *attached* to it, yet he realized that as a creature of the world he could not maintain this balance. "There was never any holy meditation, prayer, or action that I had a hand in" that succeeded, he realized. All that was left was complete submission to God. "I neither hope nor desire to stand by mine own strength, wisdom, etc., but only by faith in Christ Jesus."

But then came the miracle. Just when he had lost hope of making any spiritual progress on his own, God "filled me with such power of faith, sense of his love, etc., as has made my heart melt with joy."

This was the essence of Puritanism—the change of heart, of soul, that came when a person strove to do good, admitted his absolute failure, humbled himself before God, and, against all expectations, felt God's love and mercy. That divine love "ravished my heart with unspeakable joy." Puritans are often seen as dour and rigid, and they could be. But it was this flood of love and joy that nourished their faith.

Though the experience of God's love was life changing, it was necessarily temporary. Every time Winthrop tried to recapture the moment when he felt God's presence in his soul, it slipped away. "The more I prayed and meditated, etc., the worse I grew." A person could never demand anything from God, nor earn His favor. This was the frustrating lesson that Winthrop learned over and over again, leading him back through the cycle of seeing how arrogant he had been, how false in his resolutions, how prideful, and then, when he least expected it, experiencing the healing power of God.

GOD'S TIMETABLE

The practical effect of Winthrop's endless resolutions was to make him a careful, diligent worker who planned well to care for his family. He had to be. By the 1620s, just as his sons were growing up, his area of England was in an economic slump. Winthrop had some training as a lawyer, and as a respected landowner he presided over local courts. He left for London, where he drew the attention of leading Puritans and got a job using his legal background in the important government position of attorney of the Court of Wards and Liveries.

Winthrop had remarried again, and he was just as attached to Margaret, his third wife, as King Charles was to his queen, Henrietta Maria. Both the king and the Puritan found lifetime support and real passion in their partnerships. According to some historians, true love between husband and wife was invented at just this time. Other scholars disagree about the timing, but the history of emotions, of love and desire, of yearning and fear in this period is now considered just as important as the history of laws. The poet Thomas Carew, who wrote *The British Heaven* for King Charles, described the passionate temper of his times in a poem titled "Mediocrity in Love Rejected,"

> *Give me more love, or more disdain:*
> *The torrid, or the frozen zone*
> *Bring equal ease unto my pain,*
> *The temperate affords me none;*
> *Either extreme, of love or hate,*
> *Is sweeter than a calm estate.*

Something in the extremity of emotion that Carew described appealed to people of his day—perhaps because they sensed that they were living in an age of extremes. Winthrop's love for his wife made it all the harder for him to be in London. He pined for his family even as he lived apart from them to ensure their future. This difficult choice was just one reflection of larger changes taking place throughout the country.

In 1600 four out of every five people in England lived in the country. Those in the southern part of the kingdom, especially where the soil was rich and fertile, tended to live in small villages where everyone knew everyone else. These were far from ideal places: Scolding and gossip served to intimidate any who would stand out. This reached extremes in a practice with the strange names of "skimmington" or "riding the stang." When a husband was seen to lack control of his wife, especially if she beat him, the men of the village would gather together, lift onto a pole (or "stang") one man dressed as the weak husband and another costumed as the offending

wife, and parade the actors in front of the luckless household. In case anyone missed the point, they loudly banged on pots and pans and did their best
to shame the couple.

Yet if the village enforced conformity, it also provided basic safety and
security. These same villagers, who could be so vicious in their mockery,
also often cooperated in managing the land. The crops they grew and the
animals they raised were meant to feed everyone in the town, not to make
any single individual rich. In some villages the men got together to decide
which land to plow and when. Though one family might do a bit better than
another, over the generations things would generally even out. This pattern
could continue as long as the village stayed approximately the same size. But
England's population grew from about 3 million in 1550 to 4 million fifty

*A depiction of a skimmington by William Hogarth (1697–1764). This early work of Hogarth's was an
illustration for a book in which the main character, Hudibras, has many misadventures during his
travels. Hogarth went on to make engravings and prints that not only captured, and satirized, the people
and mood of his day but were also an important ancestor of modern comics, graphic novels, and political
cartoons.*   (COURTESY OF THE BRITISH MUSEUM)

years later, and to more than 5 million by 1650. The small-village system simply could not support all these people.

You could not miss the changes. More people needed more food, which meant more land had to be found. A company of wealthy outsiders might arrive and decide to drain a marsh that had stood near the town since beyond memory. A younger son might decide to leave to try his luck at a nearby larger town, or even in faraway London. The head of a household, like Winthrop, sometimes had to leave the village and earn a living in the big city. During the seventeenth century the population of London grew from 200,000 to 490,000. By the middle of the eighteenth century it was the largest city anywhere in Europe, including Constantinople, the capital of the Ottoman Empire. Nothing could be more different from the small village with its busybody neighbors than this city of strangers. And some farmers in the old towns where tradition had ruled for so long were reading books to decide how to get more out of their land, even if that meant discarding the ways things had always been done.

The village could not think just about taking care of its own. In a few towns, wealthier people—both locals and visitors—more ambitious, powerful people, were realizing that there was a profit to be made from so many mouths to feed. But you could not seize this opportunity if you had to spend days meeting with your neighbors and settling on whatever crop would yield just enough to go around. Instead, you had to decide for yourself what grain would sell, and specialize in that, even if it meant the village as a whole would suffer.

There was one kind of person who could do especially well in these changing times. He was one who could think carefully but act decisively, respect the past but see the future, enjoy the world but not get too attached to it. Though John Winthrop and his fellow Puritans were exactly this sort of people, they did not see the times as hopeful—in fact, just the opposite. Perhaps it was their gnawing sense that they were quite capable of turning into selfish individuals, out for themselves, that made the Puritans so determined to be purists who rejected all change.

What did these changes mean? What was the deep current moving behind the engineers altering the landscape, the departing sons, the new tensions between rich and poor? Winthrop and his Puritan friends were sure they knew. In quest stories such as *The Lord of the Rings* or *The Dark Is Rising,* there is often a moment like this, when the small village begins to sense that a great transformation is coming. Generally, someone, perhaps a wizard, knows an ancient prophecy that foretold just such a moment and warned of the days of peril to come. But there is a hope, a small band of heroes who may, just may, be able to save the day. This is precisely what the Puritans believed.

All around the Puritans the forces of darkness grew stronger. The ominous alterations in village life, breaking people away from the security of the group and pushing them out to fend for themselves, were one sure sign. On the continent of Europe, Protestants were losing horrible battles to Catholics. France and most of what is now Germany were in Catholic hands. This was another warning. England, the land chosen to protect the Protestant cause, did nothing. King Charles could not be trusted, Catholics were reentering the court, and Archbishop Laud was imposing his false religion on the people. The Catholic infiltration of England was a third and conclusive dread omen. All the signs pointed to just one conclusion: The end of days was near.

By carefully reading the Book of Revelation in the Bible, Puritans discovered what they were sure was the true pattern of human history. Centuries earlier Rome, the Pope, the Catholic Church, had stolen the teachings of Jesus and perverted them, keeping humanity enslaved. But Protestant reformers had finally risen up to combat these false prophets. Though many had paid with their lives, they were true martyrs like the early Christians. The ultimate battle between Christians and the legions of the

In this anti-Laud image, the archbishop is having a "dream," and we see all the tortures and cruelties for which he is held responsible. Laud is lying on the bed, and King Charles is at the center. The nude woman being brought to his bed is a sign of his evil, or perhaps an image of England and Ireland, which he is violating. (COURTESY OF ASHMOLEAN MUSEUM, OXFORD, AND UK/BRIDGEMAN ART LIBRARY)

Antichrist was about to begin, and England was destined to lead the forces of God. After this terrible contest the saints would rule the Earth for a thousand years. Yet England under Charles was not taking on its fated role as the homeland of the pure Protestant cause. And every day the wrath of God grew stronger.

Those who could read the signs also saw what they must do: leave the land of corruption and guide the faithful to safety in the New World. Across the Atlantic they could wait out God's punishment of England and welcome King Jesus to their purified new land. But they needed a leader, a Moses, a man who could hold them together through the journey, rally them when they reached their destination, and bind them to the true faith. Some important Puritans had noticed such a man: a devout Puritan, a successful farmer, an intelligent lawyer, a trustworthy friend. He was John Winthrop.

CHAPTER THREE

A LAND OF PROMISE

1630, SOUTHAMPTON, ENGLAND

Down to the last minute John Winthrop and many of the 1,000 people setting off for America with him were not sure that leaving England was the right decision. He was going ahead, leaving his beloved wife and family to follow once the new colony was established. Perhaps staying home to face God's judgment would be better. If the Lord was about to punish England, wasn't moving away a cowardly avoidance of duty? How could it be right to abandon friends, neighbors, family to the misguided king, his evil court, and the coming days of wrath? And even if England was no longer a good home for the faithful, what right had the colonists to enter a land already inhabited by native peoples?

As the Puritans' fleet gathered in the harbor of Southampton, Winthrop wrote out the questions people were all muttering in pri-

This portrait of John Winthrop was painted in the nineteenth century but was based on an earlier image and captures his actual appearance. Historians point out that Puritans wore black when they sat for portraits because it was a formal occasion; it was not their daily dress.
(OIL ON CANVAS BY CHARLES OSGOOD, AFTER AN UNATTRIBUTED PORTRAIT IN THE MASSACHUSETTS STATE HOUSE, COURTESY MASSACHUSETTS HISTORICAL SOCIETY, IMAGE 53)

vate. Do we have a "warrant," he wondered, to "enter upon that land which has been so long possessed by others"? The "others" he had in mind were the Narragansett, Pequot, and other native peoples the Europeans called Indians. This question of taking away land from its rightful inhabitants is not a new one. It has been raised again and again ever since 1492.

One of the most highly regarded Puritan preachers in England was John Cotton. Eventually he would move to New England, where he, Richard Mather (who married Cotton's widow), and Mather's direct descendants Increase Mather and Cotton Mather made up the heart of the religious leadership for nearly a century. John Cotton came down to Southampton to

Increase Mather. This painting from 1688 was painted during Mather's lifetime. Mather, his son Cotton, and John Winthrop were the most revered leaders of Massachusetts. Only people of their stature, and a very few wealthy individuals or couples, had their portraits painted. Unlike England, where a lively press that flourished in the absence of censorship printed many images of people and political events, New England placed much more emphasis on words than images. Even in this portrait, the books—which include The New Testament—seem as important as Mather himself.
(OIL ON CANVAS BY JOHN VAN DER SPRIET, COURTESY MASSACHUSETTS HISTORICAL SOCIETY, IMAGE 4356)

address the fears of the believers who were about to set out across the ocean. He answered all their doubts by charging them with an exceptional mission. If they were true to this path, God would aid and protect them. America, Cotton told the anxious voyagers, was a Land of Promise.

The one sure way to know that the Puritans were doing the right thing was to see it predicted in the Bible. Cotton found the perfect proof. The Bible recounts the story of the Jews fleeing slavery in Egypt, wandering in the wilderness, and then finding their destined home in Israel, the land of milk and honey. In the Second Book of Samuel (7:10) the Lord promised that "'I will appoint a place for my people Israel, and will plant them, that they may dwell in a place of their own, and move no more.'" Under the tyranny of King Charles and Archbishop Laud, the Puritans were reliving the Jews' oppression and bondage, which meant that in leaving, they were surely following God's plan. They were not cowards abandoning England; they were a chosen people on a divine mission.

What of the people already living in America? Cotton argued that as the Jews had been right to drive out the heathen Canaanites, so the Puritans were free to do the same to the Indians. In any case, the lands the Puritans intended to inhabit were now largely empty. This was true. Ever since the Spaniards had come to the Americas over a century earlier, diseases had been devastating the native populations. An epidemic that lasted from 1616 to 1619, just before the first English arrived, claimed ninety percent of the native peoples on the eastern coast of New England. Like Cotton, Winthrop thought that the fact that "God has consumed the natives with a great plague" was a sign that He intended to empty the land in order to make room for the Puritans.

This was not the only point of view the English had toward the mysterious illnesses that were consuming the native peoples. Some had a more objective, scientific approach. When Sir Walter Ralegh sent his colony to what is now Roanoke, North Carolina, Thomas Hariot had cautioned against interpreting the troubles of the natives as implying this was God's will. But in New England, where every action in the world was seen as evidence of God's plan, the conclusion seemed so obvious as to be inescapable. The only problem with this view was that if the Puritans suffered any illnesses or setbacks of their own, they knew God was angry with *them*.

According to Cotton, New England was a bountiful place, where farmers could make the land flourish and the faithful could live well. But this wonderful prophecy rested on one absolutely unbreakable condition: The godly deserved the land as long as they lived up to their promises to God. Free from the oversight of the king and his bishops, the Puritans could live exactly as God commanded, and they must do just that.

The Puritans would live promising lives in the land promised to them as long, and only as long, as they obeyed their promise to live by God's laws. If the godly failed, Winthrop predicted, "the Lord will surely break out in wrath against us, be revenged of such a perjured people, and make us know the price of breach of such a covenant."

Cotton inspired the 1,000 frightened, anxious people about to set out into the unknown with a sure sense that they were doing God's work. Throughout the history of this nation, down to the present day, many have felt that America has a special destiny: This is the homeland of freedom, of democracy, of the right of individuals to make something of themselves. There is a direct connection between John Cotton's charge to the departing Puritans and this enduring image of America as the savior of the world. But this sense of mission is also often linked to an image of America as a Protestant Christian land. The problem that quickly arose for the Puritans, and has remained ever since, is that in a land in which people could think and act as they liked, they could choose their own faiths or decide to reject religion altogether. Could a religious people allow complete freedom to disregard God's rules and still be sure they had a special place in God's plans?

On his ship the *Arbella* Winthrop tried to define more specifically how the faithful must live in the new land. He was not a preacher like Cotton, but he was writing a kind of sermon that became one of the founding documents of English life in the New World. He called it "A Model of Christian Charity."

Winthrop's model was the softest, most loving vision of a caring community imaginable. It was like the old village made perfect. Instead of Charles's *British Heaven,* in which all bow down to the king, Winthrop foresaw a community so closely woven together that all were equally important to its future. In his America, rich and poor were bonded in a very close and intimate way. The fortunate must act with "love, mercy, gentleness," while those in need must have "faith, patience, obedience." Instead of splitting people apart, their differences would actually tie them together. In practice, this vision of harmony meant that if a wealthy person lent money to an unfortunate who could not repay, he must forgive the loan.

Although Winthrop sketched out rules of behavior like this, he knew that the real basis of a godly community could not be in regulation. Rather, only "love in the heart" could give people the inner motivation to treat their neighbors as God commanded. To him Christian "love" was the necessary foundation for the colony. Every member of the community would have to "work upon their hearts by prayer, meditation . . . till . . . all in each other [are] knit together by this bond of love."

The Puritans' promise to God was that they would devote every moment of every day to living in love. Winthrop's vision of how to live this promise was inspiring. "We must be knit together in this work as one man," he preached. "We must delight in each other, make others' conditions our own, rejoice together, mourn together, labor and suffer together." We must, he wrote over and over again, love each other.

Is this possible—can love be a commandment, a regulation, a demand? Winthrop's image of a loving community required that each person, and the colony as a whole, strive endlessly toward perfection. And yet a Puritan's most basic belief was that no human being could ever escape his or her sinful nature. This was the knife edge on which Winthrop's colony must balance: Labor ceaselessly to live by God's laws, with the constant threat of His justified anger for any slips, weakness, or failings, but also know each second of each day that as weak human beings they were sure to fail again, and again, and again. Painful and difficult a challenge as this was, it also motivated the colonists to overcome every obstacle they faced.

Winthrop concluded with one of the most famous images in American history. The colony, he warned, quoting the New Testament, "shall be as a city on a hill" (Matthew 5:14). The people would be totally exposed, with the whole world watching. As Winthrop neared the New World, he was preparing his fellow passengers for prosperity at the cost of relentless vigilance, for freedom to live righteously with the knowledge that they would be constantly judged by their peers in England and by God. Both supremely confident that they were special to God and constantly anxious about whether they were living up to His trust, the Puritans guided their ships toward the new shore.

"A GREAT MARVEL"

The new land that the 400 passengers with Winthrop on the *Arbella* found waiting for them in what is now Salem, Massachusetts, was anything but promising. In fact, it was more like a cruel joke. The existing settlement at Salem was just a few homes lodged between the forest and the sea, with hardly any open land suitable for farming. Sure, there were plenty of birds in the air, fish in the water, and animals loose in the woods, but few settlers had the skill to capture them. Not only was Winthrop himself a poor shot, but the matchlock pistols of the day were so difficult to use that even an expert marksman would have a tough time.

In 1930, the three hundredth anniversary of the sailing of the Arbella, *a reproduction of the ship was built, and Frederick Winthrop sailed on it, costumed as his ancestor John. The ship no longer exists, and this photo of the celebration is one of the few surviving records.*
(COURTESY OF THE SOCIETY FOR THE PRESERVATION OF NEW ENGLAND ANTIQUITIES)

Since it was going to be hard to get food from the land, the bedraggled immigrants would have to rely on what they had brought over. But much of that had spoiled on the way, and few people had been wealthy enough to pay for transporting a cow across the ocean. If tasty game such as deer managed to stay away from the settlers, wolves were not as cautious and frequently attacked the livestock that had survived the trip.

The colonists landed in June, which meant that they did not have to cope with the cold right away. But it also meant that it was too late for planting and they would have to survive a full year on whatever they could find before any more supplies could be expected from home. Those already living in Salem warned that the winter was much more severe than in England. Here again the new land seemed to taunt the settlers rather than to provide for them. Trees were everywhere, and there were plenty of men skilled with using saws to turn timber into boards. But there were all too few men experienced with axes to do the chopping. Shelter was more likely to come in the form of Indian-style wigwams, or caves dug out of the earth. Wooden houses would have to come later.

This grim New England was a most discouraging prospect. Instead of giving the faithful a chance to live well, it reduced them to scrambling to stay alive in the most primitive conditions. And, almost at once, the deaths began. Winthrop's own 22-year-old son Henry drowned shortly after arriving. For people who were not sure it was right to leave England in the first place, this was too much, and some began to clamber back onto the ship to return home. Perhaps this colony was like the one Sir Walter Ralegh had sponsored in Virginia, and which then disappeared: a deathtrap falsely advertised as an Eden.

At just this dark moment Winthrop proved to be a great leader. Reports reaching London showed him to be a marvel of energy and confidence. He set to work building whatever was necessary with his own hands. His example was inspiring, for soon "there was not an idle person . . . to be found in the Plantation." Supposedly, even the Indians, who expected the harried English to "return as fast as they came," were impressed at how quickly they organized themselves and settled in.

Rallying the settlers to work hard and not give up was a first step. After exploring the area around Salem, Winthrop decided to move the entire group to the bay near Charlestown, a few miles away. Here there was both plenty of good land to farm and a harbor that would be easy to defend,

Another reproduction built in 1930 was of the house built in Salem for John Endicott, who arrived in 1628, two years before John Winthrop. It did not survive and was reconstructed again in the 1980s. It is part of Pioneer Village in Salem, which is struggling to find the funding to open for the public—an indication, perhaps, of the fact that the Puritans have disappeared from our sense of national history.
(HOUSE OF SEVEN GABLES)

Comparing this image of Charles and Henrietta Marie eating in their palace at Whitehall with Endicott's house in Salem gives a vivid sense of how marginal and "primitive" the colony was. At the time, the king and queen were central to England; Massachusetts hardly mattered at all. Even for a commoner such as Winthrop, the hut in which he first lived in Massachusetts was nothing like the home he left in Groton. (ROYAL COLLECTION COPYRIGHT 2003, HER MAJESTY QUEEN ELIZABETH II)

should England's Catholic enemies, the seagoing Spaniards or the nearby French in Canada, attack. Still, it was not quite the right spot, as the English could not find running water. They were not prepared to dig wells, as they superstitiously feared that the water would be unsafe. The colonists had begun to build a house for Winthrop in Charlestown, but they dismantled it, packed it up, and made a last move to what later would become Boston.

As summer faded into fall, the harsh conditions took their toll. Eleven of Winthrop's own servants died. A fierce winter that began with a gale on the day before Christmas made it worse. All told, 200 of the 1,000 persons who had left England to come to the land that God promised to them died before the first year was out. In February 1631, though, there was new hope. A ship called the *Lyon,* which had been part of the initial fleet, returned with much-needed supplies, and the weather changed. Though some more of the remaining colonists left on the ship, the worst was over.

Living now on good soil, the settlers used the spring to plant, and they could prepare better for the full year's cycle. Once word got back to England that people could indeed survive in this new land, the king did the rest. He and his archbishop made life harder and harder for the faithful. Every one of the "infectious persons" he was glad to see sail off to the New World added another settler to the Land of Promise. Unlike Virginia, which attracted single men seeking a bonanza, an El Dorado, from growing and selling tobacco, New England drew couples. From England these immigrants brought the pots, pans, gunpowder, and manufactured goods the colony could not make for itself. When they arrived, they in turn needed just what those already there had to supply: lumber, corn, and, in time, cattle.

Though too many of the first group of English settlers had died, and all had endured a terrible winter, under Winthrop's leadership those who survived were now seeing the Lord's promise fulfilled. For the incoming

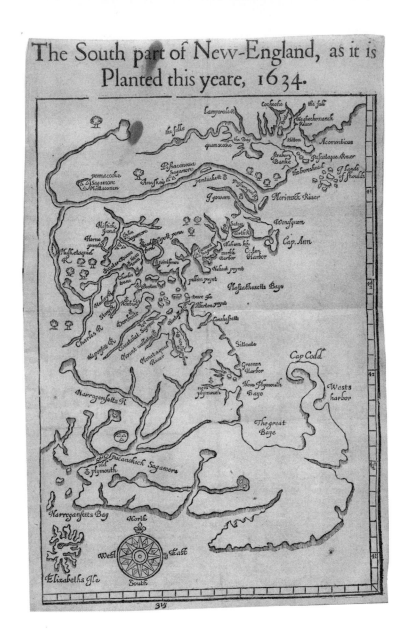

This early map shows the smattering of English settlements along the coast of New England in 1634. Like the contrasting pictures of Whitehall and Salem, it is a reminder of the limited toehold the English had in the New World. But it also shows how rapidly they spread out. With so many new communities divided by rivers and other natural barriers, people who disagreed with the policies of the Boston believers could easily set up new settlements of their own.

(WILLIAM WOOD MAP, COURTESY MASSACHUSETTS HISTORICAL SOCIETY, IMAGE 1915)

New Hampshire

Massachusetts

Connecticut River

Salem

Boston

Connecticut

Rhode
Island

Providence

Plymouth

*Narragansett
Bay*

Mystic

Saybrook

ATLANTIC OCEAN

The NEW WORLD*

*With modern state borders.

English, New England proved to be the healthiest place in the world. Fewer babies died in infancy there than anywhere else, and fully twenty percent of the first generation of men reached the age of eighty. By contrast, in the swamps of Virginia two-thirds of the first arrivals had died within five years.

John Winthrop saw his greatest reward in the fall of 1631, when his beloved wife arrived with the rest of their family. He had been right to venture forth across the seas; that was the path God intended for him. Now he and Margaret could be together again, not scrambling away from the king or cowering from the Lord's wrath, but in a land of bounty. The grateful settlers who had been inspired by Winthrop to endure the first year and who were now living well showed their appreciation. An endless parade of "fat hogs . . . venison, poultry, geese" was brought to their home. This outpouring of "joy and manifestation of love" was, he wrote, "a great marvel." The question was no longer whether they would survive, but what they would build, in the Land of Promise.

FREEMEN, AND FAITHFUL

The Puritan leaders understood contracts very well. Some, like Winthrop, had legal training. All considered their pact with God, their covenant, the most precious of all bonds, and they frequently meditated on its meaning. Many were also good businessmen, and they knew a loophole when they saw one. The king's charter for their colony did not specify where the board of directors who would run it should meet. The colonists decided to hold those sessions in New England itself, an ocean away from the king. This meant that, as long as the charter held, they were essentially self-governing—and they never had to fire a shot to win that freedom.

At first the eleven men elected leaders by the original stockholders in the colony set out to enforce Winthrop's vision of a closely bonded community by controlling prices and wages. No one should be able to take advantage of another's need, no one should be able to charge more than others could pay. Skilled workers, carpenters, and house builders could earn only eight pence more a day than they did in England. In turn, the cost of food was established by the board. The old village custom of cooperation, placing the group first, would be the new law in the new land. But with this enforced consensus, how could the other colonists have a voice?

The leaders of the colony decided that all male residents, no matter how poor, were considered freemen and could attend their meetings and elect the leaders, called "Assistants." This was the same pattern used in Virginia and in the Plymouth Plantation, but it was far more democratic than England. While Charles was doing everything to silence Parliament, the Puritan colonists showed their trust in all the faithful, even those at the bottom of the social scale. They did place limits on this rule by keeping decision-making power in the hands of the Assistants. And then they set one more key limitation: Only church members, those who had most clearly demonstrated to their neighbors that they were chosen by God, could be considered freemen.

To John Winthrop and the New England Puritans it seemed obvious: Only a society restricted to the faithful could give all men a voice. What would happen, though, if a person no longer agreed with the community about the laws of God and man? How could a loving community built in rejection of the king's laws deal with its own rebels? It was not long before Winthrop would be forced to answer this question himself.

Chapter Four

Conscience

Hearts Set upon Heaven

God was everywhere in the Land of Promise. When winter yielded to spring, it was not just a change of season, for the story of Jesus' promised return was enacted before the eyes of the faithful. As dry branches broke into leaf, wrote the poet Anne Bradstreet, "so shall it be at that great day after a long vacation, when the Sun of righteousness shall appear." The very air was crisp and clean with the promise of salvation. And the immigrants were ready—ready to hear, and see, and feel God's presence in their lives. "God's holy spirit in those days," recalled one of the early settlers, worked so directly on the "hearts of many, that our hearts were taken from old England and set upon heaven." But how should they hear, see, feel, and greet God?

Another term used for the godly, or the Puritans, was "hot Protestants"—people whose faith was so intense it burned. Believers with such fervent faith wished to serve God, yet often disagreed with each other about how to do so. Accustomed to battling against the king, against Catholics, against their own weakness, the godly expected life to be a hard fight. That struggle was often most fierce when the enemy was another burning believer.

One of the biggest conflicts came over the very kind of experience Winthrop had when he felt God's mercy and love. Which was most important—that intense sense of God's personal presence in your life? Or how you behaved before and after the onrush of joy? Even the definition of what it was like to feel God's presence varied widely. John Underhill, a Puritan in Massachusetts who would later play an important role in the war against the Pequot nation, thought his saving experience came after "the moderate use of . . . tobacco."

Those who chose the spirit sometimes came to radical conclusions. At one extreme, the godly in England included the Family of Love—a group whose name and beliefs sound like something out of the 1960s. They believed that when God revealed Himself to a person, that individual became in a sense divine and above old rules and regulations. Familists, as they were called, were accused of sharing not only their material goods but also their husbands and wives.

At the opposite end of the spectrum were preachers such as Thomas Shepard. Shepard knew many familists when he was in England and may have been tempted by their beliefs, only to become their ferocious opponent in New England. He was constantly on the alert for any sign of familism and thought it better to attack than to wait for certain proof. "A wise shepherd," he punned, "had rather let a hunter come in and kill one of his sheep than let a wolf or a fox escape."

Shepard distrusted any great emphasis on the experience of feeling God, and instead focused on very precisely defining all the stages of self-doubt, study, and good behavior a person must experience before God shows Himself. This was exactly the legalistic, rigid, performance-oriented faith that other hot Protestants in New England such as Henry Vane Jr. rejected.

A stout man whose eyes appeared to be permanently crossed, Vane has been described as looking like "a petulant child about to break into a tantrum." He came from a very powerful family. His father was one of the king's most important officials, and Vane himself had close ties to the wealthiest and most prominent of Puritan nobles. He went on to be elected governor of the new colony. Vane thought that believers who were so proud of their good actions but had not felt God personally were actually satanic and expressed their evil nature by persecuting the truly saved.

At first, the sense of being chosen people at a special moment allowed the godly in Massachusetts to debate and discuss ideas about God, spirit, and actions in the world. But when John Cotton himself arrived in 1633, this began to change. An appealing man and a captivating preacher, Cotton had a surprising message for the eager community. Though they had left England to escape from the soulless rituals of the king and his archbishop, the immigrants had not kept their faith pure. The godly were watching their neighbors' behavior, their actions, and not looking into their own hearts. They were losing sight of what really mattered—the spirit, the soul. They were becoming as dry and dead as their enemies.

Cotton's words ignited Boston like the most dynamic modern revival. Within three months of his arrival, Boston's First Church gained half again as many members as it had in three years. Winthrop himself heard the call as if he were thirsty for its message. He had been "drowsy," he suddenly real-

John Cotton, as portrayed in a nineteenth-century print based on an earlier painting. Cotton had an accepting, humane temperament that both appealed to his supporters and angered ministers such as Thomas Shepard, who suspected him of being too supportive of people with misguided, false, or harmful beliefs.

(MEZZOTINT ENGRAVING BY HEZEKIAH WRIGHT SMITH, COURTESY MASSACHUSETTS HISTORICAL SOCIETY, IMAGE 4356)

ized, and Cotton's "voice of peace" brought him back to his true knowledge of God.

Cotton was telling the faithful that all of their rules and regulations, all of their vows to love one another and to live as God commanded, were important if, and only if, they were inspired by God. Shepard heard this as the seductive voice of the Family of Love, and he was determined to expose the preacher and stamp out the infection. Vane heard a call toward the very power of the spirit Shepard distrusted.

And as more fervent believers arrived with their own views on God and man, Cotton, Winthrop, Shepard, Vane, and the rest of the believers would discover that leaving England only made the fight to live exactly as God commanded more intense, and more difficult.

THE PUREST

Sailing along with the life-saving cargo that the *Lyon* dropped off in February of that first harsh winter was a passenger who challenged the colony to live up to its beliefs. In doing so, he created a new pattern in American history. Roger Williams would accept no compromise in the Land of Promise. Either Americans fully lived up to their commitments to conscience, or they had no right to think well of their country or to claim any special place in the world. Idealists such as this do not listen to any argument based on being practical, or moderate, or even tactically clever. Anything that is not pure and right—no matter how "reasonable"—is simply wrong.

Roger Williams led the way for later crusaders of conscience such as Tom Paine, Henry David Thoreau, John Brown, Lucy Stone, Emma Goldman, and the early Malcolm X, and he did so in a colony already dedicated to living by God's laws. That made his story all the more dramatic. After all, he merely demanded of the Puritans that they take their own beliefs as seriously as he did.

When Williams and his wife, Mary, arrived in 1631, he seemed a promising addition to the community. A sweet-tempered and engaging man, his earnestness and goodness shone through everything he did. Ironically, in England the man who first recognized Williams's gifts and helped him along was Sir Edward Coke, the very spokesman for the king whom Sir Walter Ralegh had battled in his treason trial. Coke had since become a defender of some of the same kinds of rights he had opposed in Ralegh's famous case.

Trained at Cambridge University, Williams was an intelligent, committed minister—just the kind of spiritual teacher Boston needed, and the First Church offered him an official position. His response was a resounding slap in the face. Winthrop and the colonists were still members of the Church of England, even if they had put thousands of miles of ocean between themselves and Archbishop Laud and the other despicable leaders of the faith. Williams felt that he could not minister to such people. Not only was it wrong to remain attached to the Church of England, but he insisted that all the church members in Boston publicly repent for once having participated in that false and damned organization.

To Winthrop, working within the faith that most English people accepted was both necessary and generous. It was the only way to save the nation as a whole, and it meant that the godly were helping, rather than abandoning, their old neighbors and friends. That is the path every moderate leader throughout history has adopted: Hold fast to your ideals, but also keep in mind the needs of the majority, even if that compromises the most extreme, abstract principles. At some point, such leaders claim, you must choose communities run by human beings over abstract ideals, no matter how appealing those principles may be.

Williams would have none of what he condemned as "middle walking." Keeping his "soul undefiled," never having to "act with a doubting conscience," were the only things that mattered. The physical expanse of America gave him the opportunity to follow his own more extreme path. Since he would not change to fit the Boston church, and Boston would not join him in repentance, he left to find a more hospitable congregation. In England the government had enough control over the entire nation to force its opponents to leave, or to hide their true beliefs. In the America of the early 1630s crossing a few hills and rivers might be enough for you to find yourself in a place where you could believe, think, and speak as you liked.

Williams first tried nearby Salem, and the church there was eager to hire him. But Winthrop and the Boston leaders were influential enough to prevent that. Roger and Mary kept on moving and reached Plymouth. The Pilgrim colony offered an ideal home for Williams. Like him, the Pilgrims had entirely rejected the Church of England. Given a role in the local church, he threw himself into the life of the community, and Mary gave birth to their first child. Governor William Bradford appreciated him but over the course of two years began to have his own doubts. Williams, he thought, was "a man godly and zealous, having many precious parts, but very unsettled in judgment."

The old issue that arose in Boston came up again. Even Plymouth was not pure enough for Williams. After all, when members of the colony visited England, they allowed themselves to worship along with members of the Church of England. He was sure that contact with false religion must have contaminated them, and yet when they returned to America, they were again accepted into the church. This was an abomination.

Once Williams believed something, he knew he must act. As Bradford put it, he "began to fall into some strange opinions, and from opinion to practice." This was the difference between Williams and others: If he knew something to be true, consequences meant nothing.

* * *

"BOAST NOT, PROUD ENGLISH"

A man with Williams's integrity and strong criticisms of English life was not inclined to view the Narragansett who lived near Plymouth as mere heathens to be conquered. Instead, like Thomas Hariot in the Roanoke colony, he was fascinated by their language and culture. "Nature," he declared, "knows no difference between Europeans and Americans in blood, birth, bodies, etc., God having of one blood made all mankind." If any group of people was behaving in an ungodly way in America, it was the English. He chastised his countrymen in poems such as this:

> Boast not, proud English, of thy birth & blood,
> Thy brother Indian is by birth as Good.
> Of one blood God made him and thee, & all,
> As Wise, as fair, as strong, as personal.

Having seen the sinfulness of his fellow Europeans, Williams came to a startling conclusion. The rulers of Europe, including Charles, lied when they called themselves true Christians. In contrast, the Indians were good people, and they already lived on the land.

No believing Christian, Williams decided, should accept a deed to any land in America that was signed by the king. That would be a "sin of unjust usurpation upon others' possessions." All existing grants from the king must be revised to cut out any language suggesting that he had the right to give away land in the New World. The only legal and moral way to possess land was to negotiate with its rightful owners, the Indians.

This was another version of the question Winthrop had raised just before the *Arbella* left England: What right did the new settlers have to take land that was already occupied? This is one of those uneasy questions that haunts all of American history, like a family secret no one wants to discuss but everyone knows is there.

John Cotton had dismissed this concern by quoting the Bible. Williams also looked into the Bible for guidance, and he too believed that the end of time was near, that America might have a special role to play in the final days. But he drew an opposite conclusion. One of the predictions in the Book of Romans in the New Testament is that "all Israel shall be saved" (Romans 11:26). Many Puritans, like modern-day Christian fundamentalists, interpreted this to mean that shortly before the end of human history, all the Jews would convert to Christianity.

When Williams met and got to know the Indians, he thought he detected a great truth about their origins. They were, he was sure, the descendants of the ten lost tribes of Israel. These were the Jews, he thought, here in the Land of Promise, awaiting their salvation. Williams was eager to bring them to Christianity, which would save their souls and hasten the coming of a new age. But his finely honed sense of fairness began to bother him. The Puritans had not made any effort to convert natives, but—perhaps thinking of the Catholic Spanish—Williams argued that Europeans were forcing Indians to convert, or mumbling words that the natives could not possibly understand. These "monstrous and inhumane" acts were not acts of religion but of force.

If the colonists listened to Roger Williams, every one of them would be morally obligated to negotiate personally with the Indians, to cease efforts to convert them, and yet to treat them as God's chosen people.

It is not surprising that Governor Bradford and the other Plymouth leaders found Williams strange. By 1633 he was back in Salem, where he found support. But in Boston his views were no more popular than when he had left the first time. Winthrop was certainly not going to uproot the colony he had worked so hard to establish because one zealot told him to. What was worse, Williams's harsh words about the king could attract just the wrong kind of attention, endangering the special charter that gave the Puritans control of their own colony.

Still, Winthrop liked Williams and took his ideas seriously. He argued that the natives had not made use of the land on which they lived, and as long as the Puritans gave those who remained "sufficient for their use, we may lawfully take the rest, there being more than enough for them and us." Though the Puritans in Massachusetts often negotiated with the local natives and purchased from them, there is a defiant tone of bullying and greed in Winthrop's response. And yet it is impossible to imagine that the dominant view of the arriving English could have been any different. The pull of the land, and of the chance to practice their faith, was overwhelming.

However cynical Winthrop may sound, he was also right. The Europeans had advantages in skills, tools, and knowledge that allowed them to cultivate the land in new ways. If every single English colonist followed Williams's advice and either negotiated directly with the Indians or left, they would all soon be replaced by their French or Spanish rivals. Williams, with his firm conscience, was standing against the momentum of history, which did not bother him at all.

Though already in trouble with the Boston authorities, Williams continued to express controversial views. Like many religious fundamentalists in our day, he felt that women should not pray uncovered and insisted that they wear veils in church. And he thought it was wrong to force people to swear an oath that included the words "so help me God." After all, that implied God *would* help, and He alone could decide that. However, Winthrop and the other leaders of the godly colony had no intention of taking God out of the oaths they administered every day.

L IBERTY OF C ONSCIENCE

Following the inevitable course of his logic, Williams now came to another big idea; in fact, he arrived at one of the core beliefs of American life. The state, he argued, must be completely separate from the church. Today this is a cornerstone of our Constitution, but for the opposite reason. We want to protect the government from the influence of any religion, so that it is fair to all people. Williams wanted to protect religion from the government, so that it could remain pure for the saved.

Though Williams had strong supporters in Salem, his ideas were too advanced for the Puritan fathers. The Bostonians did not mind using political arm-twisting to get him out of Salem, and they informed their neighboring city that its petition to obtain more land would fail unless the Salem leaders stopped protecting him. In October 1635 Williams was officially banished from the Massachusetts colony. Since Mary was pregnant with their second child, they were given six weeks to get themselves ready to leave. They might have even more time, as long as he caused no trouble.

Williams would not let something as small as a court sentence and the risk to his family keep him quiet. He kept expressing his controversial opinions whenever visitors came to his house. By January 1636 the leaders in Boston were fed up, and they decided that banishment was not enough.

Instead, they planned to arrest him and ship him back to England, where the dissident could take his chances tangling with Archbishop Laud.

But Williams was not arrested, and he lived out his days in what would later come to be Rhode Island. That is because the same John Winthrop who rejected extreme ideas that would have destroyed his colony also rejected extreme actions that would have destroyed his opponent—and friend. He warned Williams that the jailers were coming, giving him just enough lead-time to escape. Winthrop also directed the peaceful man toward Narragansett Bay, where he stood a good chance of finding acceptance among the natives.

The first place Williams tried to build his home turned out to be within the territory of the Plymouth group, and they urged him, nicely, to keep moving. Williams finally settled in the place he called Providence, celebrating God's hand in bringing him there. True to his beliefs, he developed close contacts with the Narragansett and received a deed to the land from their leaders. He created a settlement with some friends, and by 1637 it was developed enough to welcome his wife and children, who had stayed behind in Salem. When it came time to set down rules for the growing group, Williams followed his beliefs to their final conclusion.

"We agree," the founding document of Providence read, "to hold forth liberty of conscience." The only way to protect religion from contamination was to allow freedom to all faiths. No human could be completely sure who was or was not saved, so no government should make that judgment. Instead, believers in all faiths must be free to worship as they saw fit.

Purity of faith and clarity of thought led Roger Williams to challenge the king's right to control land in America, to insist that church be kept separate from state, and, finally, to protect all faiths, even when he was sure just one was true. John Winthrop saved his colony by expelling this troubling zealot, and salved his conscience by saving his friend. They remained engaged and warm, though warmly opposed, correspondents for the rest of their lives. But even as he faced this challenge, another had arisen in Winthrop's backyard. This was an even more severe test, for Williams's ideas were so eccentric that they spoke to the future more than to his contemporaries. Anne Hutchinson, though, challenged the Puritan leaders on their own ground.

CHAPTER FIVE

SPIRIT

ANNE HUTCHINSON, "THE AMERICAN JEZABEL"

. . . thou sufferest that woman Jezebel, which calleth herself a prophetess, to teach and to seduce my servants to commit fornication, and to eat things sacrificed unto idols. And I gave her space to repent of her fornication; and she repented not. . . . And I will kill her children with death. . . .

REVELATION 2:20–23

According to Winthrop, Anne Hutchinson was "a woman of haughty and fierce carriage, of a nimble wit and active spirit, and a very voluble tongue." Like most Puritans he believed that a godly woman should be silent and obedient. Hutchinson was just the opposite, which goes a long way toward explaining why he disliked her so much. Looking at her with modern eyes, we are likely to see her as an intelligent, confident, and outspoken woman, who took her religion seriously and thought things through for herself. The problem she posed, though, was not just who she was, but what she said.

When Hutchinson arrived in Boston, she became the focus of the tensions that were already there in the community. Encouraged by Vane, she, more fully and clearly than those before her, placed spirit ahead of acts, inner life over public rules. This made her a perfect target for Shepard, who had a more dangerous opponent in Vane, for the powerful Vane threatened to use his influence with the king to revoke the Massachusetts charter if the leading ministers would not permit his view of religion to take root. Hutchinson was finally brought into court to battle against Shepard, Winthrop, and the combined wisdom of the Puritan elders. But there was also another delicate judgment hanging in the balance. For her trial tested the entire meaning of the Puritans' mission in the New World, their sacred promise to God.

Anne was the daughter of a minister, and she had been won over to Cotton's preaching in England. Most probably she came to America in 1634, with her wealthy merchant husband, William, and eleven children, to follow Cotton. Even before leaving England, she too had begun thinking about the final struggle between good and evil. Given that an ultimate battle was near, who, or which force, was the real Antichrist? Unlike Winthrop, she did not believe that Catholics were the gravest danger in the Devil's army. Ever since the Crusades some Christians had believed that Muslims were the enemy of God predicted in the Bible. Hutchinson disagreed, for there were much closer and more devilish candidates: Preachers who did not have the true spirit of Jesus "had the spirit of Antichrist." How could she detect these demons in disguise? Her conscience would tell her.

Listening to the voice of conscience is one thing; hearing voices is another. According to the surviving records, Hutchinson did more than exercise judgment when she evaluated people—she received revelations.

But this may not have been so unusual for a woman with strong convictions. The Church of England did not allow women to be preachers, so they had to find other ways to speak out. One scholar argues that Hutchinson may have known of women such as Eleanor Davis, who in 1625 announced that she "heard early in the morning a Voice from Heaven, speaking as through a trumpet these words: 'There is nineteen years and a half to Judgment Day.'"

One of Hutchinson's accusers told the court that, back in England, she said she had always known in advance about any important event in her life. On the boat coming to New England, Hutchinson apparently continued to receive messages from God. She told her daughter that she could detect whether a young man on the ship was saved or damned. She also predicted— or prophesied—that the ship had exactly three more weeks to sail, which seems to have been true.

Perhaps Anne was given to making prophecies. But her comment about the fellow on the ship also sound like a mother warning a daughter about a shipboard romance, and it is likely that all the passengers spent some time guessing how much longer they would be at sea.

Though word of these odd statements seems to have gotten out and caused some concern, Hutchinson was not only accepted into Cotton's Boston church, she began to hold informal meetings in her home. There, seated in a chair—a rare possession in Boston—she discussed Cotton's sermons with an ever-growing group of women, but soon also with women and men together. While discussion groups like this were not unusual, hers was an exception. For one thing, it was becoming very popular. For another, Hutchinson was a woman. And for a third, she began not merely to review what Cotton said but to add her own thoughts.

Viewed one way, a powerful woman, a woman who can seem quite modern in her confidence and independence, was coming into her own. Anne Hutchinson was behaving as much like a preacher as the laws of her time allowed. Her message, like Vane's, was to mistrust or condemn those deadly ministers who watched what a person *did* in the world, instead of urging the faithful to *listen* to the inner spirit. This message may have been especially appealing to women, for the inner light can come to anyone, which would mean a woman's salvation did not merely hang on her perfect, silent obedience. Instead, she could watch for signs of spirit in her own heart. Actions can be judged by the community; the spirit speaks to an individual.

It is also possible that merchants, like Anne's husband, were glad to hear a message that placed less emphasis on holding down prices, on putting community ahead of profit, and more on an inner experience that set no limits on their business practices.

Viewed in another light, a devilish woman was stepping out of her proper place by claiming to know more than anyone in the colony but Cotton and her brother-in-law, the minister John Wheelwright; by hearing voices; and by corrupting in who knows what horrible ways the simple and trusting women and deluded men around her.

By October 1636 Vane's group, including Hutchinson and her followers, were so numerous that they made a move to add Wheelwright on as a third pastor at the Boston church. This split the church between those who thought one's actions mattered and those who cared only about the inner spirit. A battle over church offices was turning into a contest over who spoke for the true faith. Even as both sides grew more heated, the Puritan leadership sought a way to reconcile them. A day of fasting was called in January 1637 so all could examine their consciences, and Wheelwright was invited to speak. This was a disastrous choice.

Wheelwright preached spiritual war. "We must kill," he urged. "Kill them with words of the Lord." He did not mean murder, but he did mean to battle, defeat, replace all those who did not emphasize the inner spirit. This was a direct challenge to every other minister in the colony, and they heard it. Over the course of the year Winthrop defeated Vane in a new gubernatorial election and Vane returned to England, Wheelwright was tried and banished, a meeting of ministers defined the official religious beliefs of the colony in terms that Cotton reluctantly accepted, and Hutchinson herself was brought to trial. There were a variety of charges, but they amounted to an accusation that under the guise of teaching the word of God, she was subverting the colony, attacking its leaders, and spreading discord.

Trial

John Winthrop, as governor of the colony, ran the trial. "We must be knit together in this work as one man," he had urged while on the *Arbella*. How would he now face one woman who threatened to unravel that fabric, to place the personal voice of what—conscience, spirit, God?—ahead of all others. This was the test: How could "must" and "love" govern together? Not well.

Winthrop's opening statement sounds hauntingly like something out of George Orwell's *1984,* or an account of a prisoner being "reeducated" during China's Cultural Revolution. Winthrop sent for Hutchinson so that "we may reduce you that so you may become a profitable member here among us." "Reduce" had two meanings at the time. The main sense (rooted in the Latin *ducere,* "to lead") was to "lead back," as one would bring a wandering child back to the path. But the more modern implication was there too: to cut down, even to silence.

"I am called here to answer before you," Hutchinson protested, "but I hear no things laid to my charge." Though she had no legal training, she was an able advocate, and kept challenging the terms under which she was being tried.

John Winthrop: "Why for your doings, this you did harbor and countenance . . . this faction."
Anne Hutchinson: "That's a matter of conscience, sir."
John Winthrop: "Your conscience you must keep or it must be kept for you."

This last sentence was the fatal challenge of the Land of Promise. In twelve words Winthrop predicted the failure of the Puritan vision of America and, more generally, the irresolvable contradiction at the heart of any government based on a religious faith.

"Conscience" in the seventeenth century was not seen as an individual matter—a prompting that might vary from person to person. Rather, it was closer to its root, "consciousness," an inner awareness of the universal and perfect laws of God. Yet who determines what those laws are? If we are a godly community, the community together monitors how well we adhere to His laws. But is that conscience? How does it differ from the very kind of top-down order King Charles saw as his British Heaven? To save his settlement of spirit-drunk Puritans, Winthrop spoke as a bully, a tyrant, by silencing spirit and insisting on conformity.

Winthrop pressed Hutchinson on her meetings. What gave her the right to hold them, to speak to men? She pointed to the passage in the New Testament in which older women are instructed to teach younger ones. He could not disagree, and the more he tried to trap her, the more foolish and blundering he seemed, until all he could do was retreat behind his authority as a male: "We do not mean to discourse with those of your sex."

If she shouldn't be speaking out to others, she chided, "Why do you call me to teach the court?" And what rule, she demanded to know, had she broken? Unable to name any such regulation, Winthrop pouted: "I have brought more arguments than you have."

Winthrop suspected that Hutchinson's meetings were far from religious. Over and over he used the word "seduce" to describe ways she might have misled the "simple souls" who came to listen to her. In a second trial the following March, Hutchinson's judges made clearer what at least one meaning of the word "seduce" implied. They claimed that her views were a disguised argument for sexual orgies. Through Hutchinson, they implied, the Family of Love was trying to spread its vile doctrines in God's chosen land. This was a complete fantasy, but that didn't make it any less real to the judges. Perhaps this too-forward woman, who dominated her own husband, was telling other women to ignore the bonds of marriage. If old English villagers mocked couples in which the wife acted the part of the husband, in New England such marriages were suspected of harboring heresy.

The problem Hutchinson posed was not, or not just, that she held meetings, it was that she used those gatherings to spread her beliefs. She was now accused of being the source of all of the colony's problems.

THOMAS DUDLEY, DEPUTY GOVERNOR: "About three years ago we were all in peace. Mrs. Hutchinson . . . hath made a disturbance. . . . She hath been the cause of what is fallen out."

If they exiled her, everyone would be calm again.

Thomas Dudley: "We must take away the foundation and the building will fall."

Given the conflicts with Roger Williams that were going on in just this period, Dudley had a very selective memory. Still, important ministers were brought in to report on Hutchinson's most extreme criticisms. Had she claimed that all those trained and worthy men did not deserve to be preachers? Did she accuse the most godly ministers in God's Promised Land of being the forces of the Antichrist?

Thomas Shepard: "I remember she said that we were not able ministers of the New Testament."

Five more prominent men had similar recollections. Hutchinson debated with them on the particulars of what she had said, how severe in judgment she had been. This went on for some while to little effect, and Winthrop finally decided to adjourn for the night.

The next day Hutchinson tried a bold new approach. She demanded that the six ministers swear under oath that their recollections of conversations with her were accurate. Puritans took oaths extremely seriously. If a believing Puritan had the slightest doubt about anything he said, he could not vouch for it under oath. Since the ministers were all recalling conversations from nearly a year earlier, it was close to impossible for them to have the level of certainty about every detail an oath required.

With this brilliant challenge Hutchinson took over the trial. The focus was no longer on her words but on the ministers who seemed hesitant and weak. Her liberty was being weighed against accusers who would not swear to tell the truth. This may have heartened some of her supporters, for they began to speak up. One of them mentioned the person whose presence loomed behind the whole trial: He requested that John Cotton come and give his judgment. If Cotton defended Hutchinson, the entire case could collapse.

Cotton was very good at saying two things at once. That was how he managed to be the hero to Hutchinson and her group and still remain in the good graces of the other ministers. In court he did the same, until finally he had to come down on one side. He agreed with Hutchinson. He did not believe she had been as harsh on the ministers as they claimed.

At this moment the case could have ended. And just at this moment it radically changed. That is why at least one modern historian questions the record. It was just too perfect for Winthrop and the battered judges. And yet what followed was not out of keeping with Hutchinson's reported beliefs. Hutchinson set out to explain how she knew which ministers were good and which ones bad, how she could separate the forces of good from those of the Antichrist.

"Now if you do condemn me," she finished up, "for speaking what in my conscience I know to be truth I must commit myself unto the Lord."

INCREASE NOWELL (an officer of the court): "How do you know that that was the spirit?"
ANNE HUTCHINSON: "How did Abraham know that it was God that bid him offer his son?"
THOMAS DUDLEY: "By an immediate voice."

ANNE HUTCHINSON: "So to me by an immediate revelation."

THOMAS DUDLEY: "How! An immediate revelation."

ANNE HUTCHINSON: "By the voice of his own spirit to my soul."

Anne Hutchinson was speaking as Joan of Arc, as Eleanor Davis—the Englishwoman who had heard the voice of the Lord—but also as one condemned. She had given the court exactly what it wanted, proof that her ideas about the spirit had gone too far. A woman hearing voices from God was surely misguided, or worse. She was no wise teacher of truth but a mouthpiece of error.

THOMAS DUDLEY: "I am fully persuaded that Mrs. Hutchinson is deluded by the Devil, because the spirit of God speaks truth in all his servants."

OF MONSTROUS BIRTHS

After her admission in court, the colony leaders had little difficulty in banishing Hutchinson from New England. The world confirmed their judgment. Hutchinson had been pregnant during the trial. But what she gave birth to was nothing human. It was a clot that seemed to hold thirty monstrous stillbirths within it. There is a modern medical explanation for such an abnormality. But to Winthrop it was simply a proof, divine evidence, of the equally vile beliefs she was trying to bring to life in the colony. God was punishing her and showing all the world who she truly was.

Five years later, when they were living in rural Pelham Bay, New York,

Anne Hutchinson and everyone in her family except one were killed in an Indian raid. As Revelation had predicted, Jezebel's children had been killed. A perfect case, the Massachusetts fathers were sure, of divine justice.

Hutchinson may have believed she heard voices. Perhaps she was deluded. Perhaps she used such phrases to give her, a woman, a way to speak her mind. It may even be that the trial record is not accurate, and that her sole crime was in being a forthright woman who challenged men on their own terms. But the case was never just about one woman—it was also about how the colony would balance the fervent inner voice against rules and regulations of outward behavior.

In condemning Hutchinson and celebrating their victory, Winthrop succeeded in resolving the conflict between spirit and actions. Shepard preached a new path in which each day you made small improvements in your life—guided, to be sure, by the spirit of God. To this day many Americans tell themselves that "every day in every way I am getting better and better." They are following Shepard's plan. For the Puritans, living a good life had become a good sign, a very strong sign, that you were saved. And no inner spirit could overrule that constant effort.

Yet in gaining control of one woman, and of their colony, the leaders also lost. Vane left, Cotton was tamed, there was much less room for hot Protestants to find and describe God in their own ways. The ministers silenced a voice of passion that spoke for the unbridled spirit that had been the deepest source of their whole movement. In the same way, exiling Williams had preserved the charter and the rule of the faithful by removing the colony's most devout and most uncompromising believer. Conformity to the group now overruled the individual conscience.

Could it have been any other way? Perhaps not. Dudley pointed out during the trial that if every revelation were accepted, there would be constant war, since each prophet would refuse to listen to any outside authority. Could any community devoted to God accept every possible interpretation of His meaning? Honor every speaker who claimed to hear His voice? Living in the Land of Promise was causing the Puritans to refine and reconsider their pact with God. But what then of the Indians? Neither Williams's idealism nor Winthrop's bland assurance that there was room enough for all could answer that question. That required guns and blood, and another adjustment of God's mission for the faithful.

CHAPTER SIX

WAR

HOGGERY

To this day no one can fully explain why the Puritans behaved so savagely in their war against the Pequot people. By crushing the Pequot, the Puritans gained control of good land and key trade routes. Perhaps that is enough of a reason. As the Massachusetts men searched what is now southern Connecticut for new places to settle, one Pequot left a record of what this invasion looked like to him. An Englishman quoted him as saying, "What Englishman, what cheer, what cheer, are you hoggery, will you cram us?" Across the static of this record of half English there is a clear sense of threat: "Will you cram us?"—do you intend to force us off the land? But there seems to have been more to the Puritans' fury than even greed.

One recent view is that these hot Protestants were so accustomed to doing battle for God, even against each other, that they needed to invent a new enemy. They had to believe that the Land of Promise contained evil forces who would try to prevent God's chosen people from fulfilling their destiny. As a result, they turned nearby native people into their own image of devils, and set out to destroy them with the anger of the righteous. The commission given to John Mason, one of the leaders of the Puritan military campaign, certainly sounds that way. He was instructed "to execute those whom God, the righteous judge of all the world, hath condemned for insulting his sacred majesty . . . make their multitudes fall under your warlike weapons . . . your feet shall be set on their proud necks."

The Puritans were ready to fight, but why against the Pequot? By the mid-1630s the English were moving up the Connecticut River, expanding their trading posts and settlements. This brought them into conflict with other Europeans, including the Dutch, based in what is now New York, and the Plymouth Pilgrims. Just at the same time, native nations in the area such as the Pequot, the Narragansett, the western Niantic, and the Mohegan were going through their own period of shifting alliances. Each European group presented a native nation with a potential ally or enemy, and precisely the same was true in reverse. All of these calculations fostered an environment of treachery and suspicion, misunderstanding and vengeance, made all the worse because the Europeans claimed not to be able to tell one native group from the other, and the natives said exactly the same about the Europeans.

An unpleasant, often drunken, abusive English smuggler named John Stone was the unlikely spark that turned tension and hostility into blazing war. Stone was sailing on the Connecticut River in a small trading boat with a captain and a six-man crew when he kidnapped two natives to use as guides. These men were most probably Niantics, who were allies of the Pequot. But Stone's group was being followed by other natives, perhaps both Pequot and Niantic, who attacked them at night, blew up the ship, and killed all of the English. The natives were not merely freeing the two guides but taking revenge for a Pequot leader who had been recently captured by the Dutch and held for ransom. Even though the natives paid the price, the Dutch murdered him.

When they learned of the attack, the Massachusetts leaders demanded that Stone's killers be turned over to them, and that the Pequot pay significant damages. Both the Europeans and the natives used wampum—specific varieties of whelk or clam shells strung together on strings—as currency. The very area that was now in dispute was crucial to the manufacture and distribution of these shells. But the natives felt that their assault on Stone was justified, both by his actions and by the treachery of the Dutch. The fact that Stone was English did not make any difference to them.

In the Puritan imagination, Stone's murder and the Pequot's refusal to make amends was no small matter; it was a sign of the savagery of their diabolical enemy. The Puritans set out to do God's work and punish the evildoers. It is this escalation that is so hard to understand, for their response to one attack was all-out, brutal war.

As the Puritans readied their forces, the Pequot looked for allies and approached the Narragansett to side with them. Even though he had been exiled from Boston, and was protective of the Narragansett people, Roger Williams rowed "thirty miles in great seas, every minute in hazard of life," to argue against the Pequot and to urge the Narragansett leaders to align with the English. Williams won that argument.

The Narragansett were concerned, though, about how the English might conduct themselves in war. They must have heard rumors of English savagery, and they wanted to be sure that only men, warriors, would be attacked. As Williams reported, "It would be pleasing to all natives that all women and children be spared." They were not.

SEVERE JUSTICE

War in Europe was a matter of terror as well as conquest. If you showed your enemy only once how destructive you could be, he would be likely to surrender and avoid future combat. This "severe justice" was the strategy Sir Walter Ralegh had used in Ireland when he had participated in, and may have helped to lead, a massacre at Smerwick. This was not how the Pequot had fought in the past. In skirmishes, the Pequot did their best to terrify and humiliate the English. They tortured captives near the English camp, so their screams could be heard. Then they taunted their enemy, calling them women whose god was nothing but an insect. The Pequot also kidnapped women and children, though it seems they treated their captives well. But when the English refused to reassure them that there would be only limited combat, the warriors swore that they would be willing to attack women and children too. The English struck first.

Near what is now Mystic, Connecticut, a force led by captains John Mason and John Underhill came upon two Pequot villages surrounded by wooden stakes. Both were well defended, but one held women and children. The English and their Narragansett allies surrounded the one that housed the noncombatants, killed as many of the warriors, women, and children as they could, then burned what remained to the ground. As many as 700 people may have been killed.

The Pequot lost the war, and the English did their best to make sure they would be no threat ever again. Their leaders were shipped off to the West

Indies as slaves, while many of the remaining Pequot were sent to live with, and blend into, other tribes. But once again the actual experience of living in America had called into question the Puritans' mission from God.

The Puritans' Indian allies protested the massacre, saying it was "too furious, and slays too many men." Underhill himself understood that this

This picture of the destruction of the Pequot fort in Mystic gives a sense of the ferocity of the battle. The English and their Narragansett allies are depicted as the wheels of a machine grinding down the fort. In the center, guns blast at Pequots even as they run away. Unfortunately, very few artifacts and almost no other images of the Pequot from this period have survived.

(COURTESY OF THE JOHN CARTER BROWN LIBRARY AT BROWN UNIVERSITY)

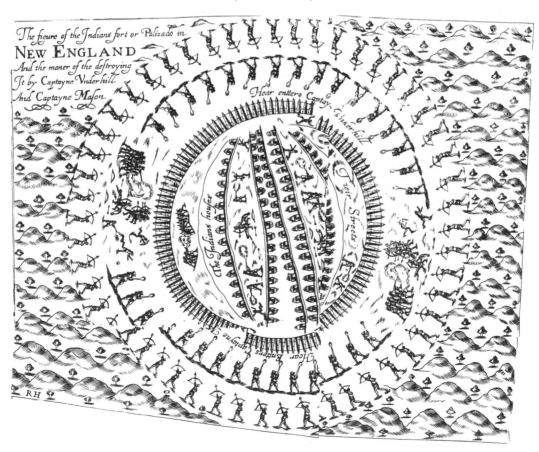

was a troubling issue. "Should not Christians have more mercy and compassion?" he questioned. His chilling answer was one that Cotton had given back in England: In the Bible, God supported wars fought by leaders such as King David. When God punishes a sinful people, He "harrows them, and saws them, and puts them to the sword, and the most terriblest death that may be." The success of the war was proof—God had been on their side.

The Puritans arrived in the Land of Promise eager to live godly lives. Within a decade of their arrival they had accomplished a great deal: They controlled ever more land and had defeated nearby native nations. Troublesome believers such as Williams and Hutchinson were banished. Vane left on his own, and both Wheelwright and Cotton were tamed. But there was a price for this success. The godly now saw their neighbors as savages and their most radical thinkers as heretics. The battle for God in the new land, it seemed, would ultimately be won only when all of the devilish enemies had been destroyed. And yet that is not the whole story. Protected by Winthrop, Williams did survive. While soldiers burned Pequot women and children, Williams adopted a Pequot boy.

In England, Puritan believers spoke out against what they saw as an evil government. Now, in the new land, the Puritan government was becoming ever more established, while a few believers challenged its laws and actions. The legacy of the Puritans was both centuries of war that left native peoples with almost none of the land they had once inhabited, and fervent critics of those policies who continue to be heard to this day. Perhaps becoming so rigid and domineering was the only way the Puritans could have survived and prospered. But what, then, was the real promise of America? And where could a searching soul find a true Heaven on Earth? Surprisingly, the answer seemed to be thousands of miles away, in England, where the true and final battle between Good and Evil was taking shape.

MEN ON
HORSEBACK

CHAPTER SEVEN

"No Small Evils"

1637

Archbishop Laud was worried. Writing to Thomas Wentworth, the man Charles had entrusted with governing Ireland and who was soon to be named the first Earl of Strafford, he confided, "My misgiving soul is deeply apprehensive of no small evils coming on. . . . I can see no cure without a miracle." The archbishop and the earl soon found out how very much in need of a miracle they were. King Charles's British Heaven was in the gravest danger, and Puritans on both sides of the Atlantic believed the turning point of human history had arrived. The kingdom of the saints on Earth might begin in England after all.

The crisis began in Scotland. Since Charles was the ruler of Scotland, he believed that he should be able to choose the prayer book to be used in Scottish churches. Of course it should be the

Book of Common Prayer, which had been created for the Church of England, altered slightly for Scottish taste. On July 23, 1637, the new book was used for the first time in the very church where Charles had been crowned King of Scotland. The congregation rebelled. Believing the word of God was being defiled, Scottish men and women turned services into riots. To the Scots the new prayers were everything horrible rolled into one, they were "heathenish, Popish [Catholic], Jewish."

There was a key difference in the way Protestantism was practiced in England and in Scotland. The Church of England was directly responsible

Scots in St. Giles Cathedral, Edinburgh, rioted when the new prayer book was read on July 23, 1637.
(COURTESY BRITISH LIBRARY, LONDON, AND UK/BRIDGEMAN ART LIBRARY)

to the king. In addition, like the Catholic Church, it was governed by richly adorned bishops and other high officials. Running a church with a strict hierarchy of deacons, priests, and bishops is called an Episcopal system, and thus in America believers in this brand of Christianity are Episcopalians (in England today they are called Anglicans; Anglican simply means English, a member of the Church of England). The Scots preferred a form of church government in which rules were established by conferences of presbyters, or elders, from all the churches. Once these policies were set, they were tightly enforced. Not surprisingly, this is called Presbyterianism.

Why should church structure matter so much? Bishops versus presbyters hardly seems like something to fight about. The conflict between England and Scotland was not a small issue of how to organize the faith; it was about its very nature. Each country believed it needed to have one single, national church for the whole nation. If you believed that a misguided king was imposing false beliefs and empty rituals on you, your very soul was in danger. In turn, if you believed that rebellious hotheads were defying the divinely ordained king, the entire security of the kingdom was at stake.

Once again top-down rule was being challenged, this time not by individual Puritans but by an organized faith that united an entire country. One bishop in Scotland, realizing the threat, placed two loaded pistols in front of him as he preached, and he stationed his armed wife and servants in front of the lectern to warn and silence his congregation. Charles merely told his advisers to imprison the protesters. This was simultaneously arrogant and ignorant.

Nothing could do a better job of uniting the Scots than having the king of England impose religious rules on them. In February 1638 leading nobles and ministers, city dwellers and country squires, gathered together and signed a National Covenant. They all swore their opposition to "our poor country being made an English province." Copies of the agreement were carried all over Scotland to rally support, and thousands of Scots signed their names to them.

Charles was now in a terrible spot. He hated the Scots' defiance, which seemed like a rebellion against his authority. *"I will rather die,"* he practically screamed in a letter, "than yield to their *impertinent* and *damnable* demands." But what could he do? In order to be a true king, he would have to enforce his religious rule in Scotland. There were only two ways he could do that: bring over soldiers from Ireland or gather them in England.

Though Charles seriously considered the option of using Irish Catholics to enforce obedience from Scottish Protestants, he took what must have seemed like the less risky course: He relied on his English subjects to rally to their faithful ruler and bring order to their unruly neighbors. This was a double failure.

In the time it took for Charles to gather 20,000 raw troops and march them to the border of Scotland, the Scots purchased arms, found a seasoned, capable general in Alexander Leslie, and occupied every strategic hill and impregnable castle. Even Charles recognized that this was a hopeless position and backed off. He used all his charm to convince the Scots he was an agreeable sovereign, and one negotiator was struck by what a "just, reasonable, sweet person" Charles was. He was wrong.

Charles was perfectly willing to tell an opponent anything, but only in order to buy time. He wrote that "there is a Scots proverb that bids you to put two locks on your door after you have made peace with a foe," and he meant it. He never intended to concede anything. Instead, he thought that this moment of national crisis was a good time to call Parliament. And in that he was the one who was wrong.

For eleven years Charles had ruled without his legislators. But now he must get those religion-mad, conspiratorial, king-hating men to give him money. Though Parliament was willing to discuss money, it had other things on its mind. The king knew perfectly well the issues that bothered Parliament, and he offered to end that hated tax, ship money, in exchange for a large one-time payment. Three years after he had won the court ruling that made him master of the law, he was backing down to the very lawyers who had opposed him. The legislators pressed their advantage, demanded more concessions, and were planning to issue a proclamation against war with Scotland when Charles once again dissolved Parliament.

The one man who completely shared the king's views, and his confidence, was Strafford. If Parliament would not obey the king, ignore it, he counseled. After all, "you have an army in Ireland you may employ here to reduce this kingdom. One summer well employed will do it." Just as Winthrop had glowered at Hutchinson, threatening to "reduce" her, Strafford glared at all England, insisting that he could bring it to heel.

The earl was given his chance, for on August 18, 1640, he was made commander in chief of the army. For all his strong will, he was not the most compelling of figures: Wracked with gout, his vision blurred, he was carried into battle on a stretcher. Ten days later the 25,000 Scottish soldiers under Leslie turned south and entered England. This was a very unusual invasion. The troops were extremely disciplined, and unlike most soldiers in their day, they did not steal as they marched. There was a good reason for this: Even as they moved through England, they were in constant contact with a key group in the very land they were conquering. Former members of

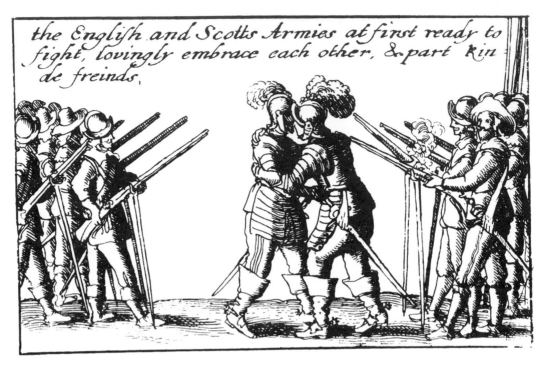

the English and Scotts Armies at first ready to fight, lovingly embrace each other, & part kinde freinds,

English and Scots armies behaving more like friends than enemies.   (THE FOTOMAS INDEX)

Parliament who disliked the king's brand of Protestantism were secretly plotting with the Scots. If this was war, it was not merely Scotland against England but rather the beginning of a civil war that would splinter both kingdoms. "No small evils," indeed.

"I CANNOT DEFEND A BAD, NOR YIELD A GOOD CAUSE"

Charles was like a chess player who always has one more move planned—a secret escape route for his key pieces, no matter how cornered they seem to be. But for him those last moves always made a very bad situation worse. He never learned from his mistakes or recognized his own willful pattern of behavior.

Why was Charles so obstinate, able to offer seeming concessions solely when he did not mean them, never really accepting any outcome other than total victory, even if that meant, over and over again, that he suffered increasingly devastating defeats? One answer may lie in his childhood relationship to his brother Henry. Called "the flower of the house, the glory of the country," Henry was a charmer and won "the admiration of all strangers."

Charles was the opposite: He suffered from rickets, had weak bones, and had trouble standing. At his formal introduction to court he was flanked by two nobles, in case he collapsed. Through endless effort and great force of will he made himself into an excellent horseman, hunter, and even runner. As a child he was shy, awkward, and not attractive. His one means of getting attention from his distant father, King James, was by fawning on him, a strategy he also tried with his glorious brother. Just one reliable story about the two brothers has survived, but it is revealing. We know that as a teenager Henry made fun of Charles for his softness and appearance, and Charles ran off in tears. The stutter Charles developed may have been an indication of his anger at this cold family that revolved around a tyrant the world loved.

When Henry died, Charles took his place in the line of succession, but he was never beloved as his brother had been. It may be that the unappreciated son, who grew up in his brother's shadow, who struggled to control his body, and who was finally paid attention only when he became the royal heir, is the key to Charles the king. He stubbornly mastered himself, so he stubbornly resisted others. The only alternative to being a king by the right of God was to be the boy nobody liked, so he could never accept any diminution of his power. He had hated his family and lived by flattery, so he was gracious in negotiations only when he was sure he would eventually crush his opponents.

This "triple portrait" of Charles was painted by the noted Flemish painter Anthony Van Dyck. It was a study meant to guide the equally famous Italian sculptor Bernini in creating a bust of the king. Charles knew some of the best European artists of his time, and his lavish court supported them. The Bernini head has not survived, and the painting is now an interesting portrait of Charles, the man who wanted to be a kind of sculpture, a symbol of wisdom, righteousness, and authority to his people.

In the face of the Scottish invasion, the move left to Charles was to call Parliament again and to stick it out with them. Stick it out they did, for the Parliament he summoned in November of 1640 remained in session for the rest of his life.

The leadership of the House of Commons was a nightmare for the king. At the center stood John Pym; fervently anti-Catholic and an extremely able politician, he organized the secret dealings with the Scots. Next in command was John Hampden, the very man who had brought the ship money case against the king. Hampden's lawyer in that case was another leading Puritan legislator, Oliver St. John. A much more obscure member of Parliament was related by marriage to both Hampden and St. John, and may well have owed his seat to his family connections and his religious beliefs. Noticed first for his plain country clothes and fervent style of speaking, that man was Oliver Cromwell.

The king had gotten his way for a decade, trampling on what the legislators saw as their rights. Now that he needed Parliament's support, his enemies could name their price. The religious radicals in the House of Commons used their newfound strength to pass a law sending groups out to complete the destruction of all the images in English churches, which had begun in Elizabeth's time. The shattering of beautiful stained-glass windows and the smashing of sculptures of Jesus was as much the sound of a righteous Parliament as the speeches about liberty and conscience.

The legislators took aim at Archbishop Laud, at the judges who had ruled against Hampden in the ship money case, and against the Catholics whom Charles had tolerated or protected; and they went out to get Strafford. One after another, these men were imprisoned and tried for treason.

Charles was desperate to protect Strafford, his most effective and loyal friend. Charles swore that "upon the word of a king you shall not suffer in life, honor, or fortune." He tried everything, even offering Pym a high post at his side, to make good on his oath. When this failed, Charles attempted one of his typically disastrous last-minute moves, letting out word that he intended to send soldiers to storm the jail and free Strafford. He hoped that this threat would cause Parliament to back off. The king's combination of intimidation and weakness did just the opposite.

Crowds howled through London, demanding Strafford's death. And more—the enemy was not just one man, it was the Catholics, the queen, the Irish. These forces of evil were everywhere and had to be destroyed. Under siege, Charles faced a new impossible choice—go back on his word as a king, or put his own wife and family in danger. Though he regretted it for the rest of his life, Charles sacrificed Strafford and his word for Henrietta Maria and his heart.

On May 12, 1641, the one man who had been able to control Ireland was executed. This did not calm the mood of the city. Panic and fury over Charles's threat to use force, fear and hatred of Catholics—all carefully inflamed by Pym—made for an electric atmosphere. And then in late October the most terrifying rumors of all began to cross the water from Ireland: Armed with a commission from the king to kill all Protestants, Irish Catholics were murdering the faithful in their beds, pushing men and women off bridges and watching them drown, slaughtering 10,000—or was it 100,000 or 150,000?—of their defenseless neighbors. Thousands of Protestants crowded English ports, escaping from the horror, each adding a new tale of savagery and blood. Like America in September 2001, England was facing terror on a scale it had never experienced.

Though there was no commission from the king, the rumors were not entirely false. A rebellion did break out in Ireland, and perhaps 3,000 Protestants were killed. The real causes were conflicts among the factions in Ireland, which had many sources but soon spread out of control. To radical Protestants in England, though, this was not a local matter at all. The evil forces of Catholicism were beginning their long-predicted campaign to take back the true Protestant land. The final battle between the saints and the Antichrist, which both Winthrop and Hutchinson had seen coming, had begun.

Unable to impose his prayer book on the Scots, unable to protect his loyal general in England, unable to control the blood-stained island of Ireland, Charles now faced opponents who believed they were the attacking arm of God.

When Stephen Marshall preached a sermon to the House of Commons, he turned to the Bible. God's word spoke for war, for ruthless, unblinking, final war. Starting from the Book of Judges, he preached, "God's meanest servants must not be afraid to oppose the mighty." Don't be afraid to attack the king, he implied. He cited the bloodcurdling Psalm 137, "Happy shall he be, that taketh and dasheth [Babylon's] little ones against the stones." Don't be afraid to kill without mercy. And he used the words of Jesus himself as a bloody challenge, "He that is not with me is against me" (Matthew 12:30 and Luke 11:23).

The only option left for Charles was to attack first. When Pym organized Parliament to send the king a Grand Remonstrance—a long list of all of his failings—Charles decided to respond with force.

On January 3, 1642, the king's attorney general indicted Pym, Hampden, three other members of the opposition, and one lord for treason. England's Parliament is divided into two sections, the House of Commons and the House of Lords. The legislators disappeared before they could be jailed. The next day, though, the five members of the House of Commons appeared as usual, seemingly waiting to be arrested. No king had ever entered Parliament with armed men, but Charles and his soldiers set out to take the rebels in.

As Charles neared the building, a captain loyal to Parliament rushed to warn the five, who had planned the whole day to trap the king into making a blundering show of force. They dashed through a back door and slipped off in a waiting boat. Charles arrived just a few minutes later to see that "the birds have flown." He assured the remaining members that he would try the men "in a legal and fair way." No one believed him. As the great poet and passionate Puritan John Milton put it, "If some vulture in the mountains could have opened his beak intelligibly and spoke, what fitter words could he have uttered at the loss of his prey?"

Over the next few months king and Parliament gathered their forces, and by late summer they were ready to face off in open battle.

Chapter Eight

"A Rebellion Against Us and the Law"

Melancholy

In a civil war each side has to scramble to find sources of money, for until one group wins, the usual systems of finance no longer exist. While the king could count on wealthy nobles, Parliament controlled the city of London, which gave it access to fortunes made in trade. Charles knew that the universities of Oxford and Cambridge possessed significant stores of money and valuable metal, and in July he asked for these riches to be sent to him. Learning of this, Oliver Cromwell hurriedly gathered a couple of relatives, raised some men, and rushed off to make sure the king would not get anything from Cambridge. He and his band blocked the main roads and captured Cambridge Castle, which had its own supply of money and ammunition. In this small sortie, the unheralded member of Parliament with

no military training revealed the bold determination and quick thinking that would make him great.

To this day Cromwell is the most controversial figure in British history. It is as if presidents Abraham Lincoln and Jefferson Davis, generals Ulysses S. Grant and Robert E. Lee, the merciless William T. Sherman and the murderous John Wilkes Booth, were combined into one person. How you judged Cromwell depended entirely on which side of the English Civil War you favored. Given that people have felt so strongly about him for three and a half centuries, it is not surprising that there are many legends and stories about his youth. His supporters love to recount moments that proved he was destined for greatness. His enemies counter with tales showing that his cruel and calculating nature was apparent from childhood on. Modern historians do not trust any of these stories.

In fact, Cromwell was one of those people who discover themselves in action. We know much more about what he *did* than who he really *was*. But that fits a view he had of himself. Believing that everything he accomplished was as an agent of God, he said, "No one rises so high as he who knows not whither he is going." To his critics this was pure deception. He knew very well where he was going—on a single-minded quest to destroy the king and take his place. The more interesting possibility is that he really meant it. That then leaves it to us to explain what enabled him to become a great man, when he himself did not know.

Cromwell came from a background somewhat similar to Winthrop's. "I

Opposite: *The Tree of Life is a kind of map of forces that believers in the Kabbalah—a brand of Jewish mysticism—study. In this anti-Cromwell illustration, the artist has adapted the Tree of Life into a chart proving that Cromwell was the Antichrist.*   (The Fotomas Index)

Oliver Cromwell reportedly insisted to a painter that he "paint my picture truly like me and flatter me not at all. But [pointing to his own face] remark all these roughness, pimples, warts and everything as you see me. Otherwise I will never pay a farthing for it." (quoted in Cromwell, Our Chief of Men, *p. 472.) This unfinished painting by Samuel Cooper is thought to be the most accurate image of him. The gruff, plain-talking Cromwell was the perfect opposite of Charles, who used the best artists in Europe to turn himself into a symbol of royal rule.*   (PRIVATE COLLECTION AND UK/ BRIDGEMAN ART LIBRARY)

was by birth a gentleman," he once explained, "living neither in any considerable height, nor yet in obscurity." Like the Winthrops, the Cromwells obtained most of their property when Henry VIII sold off church lands. The main difference in the two Puritan leaders' backgrounds is that while Winthrop's family was slowly accumulating land and wealth, Cromwell's was in decline. But although his own family struggled, Cromwell's broader network of relations included wealthy and powerful men. One way to explain his determination is to see him as a marginal outsider in an otherwise successful family. Perhaps the constant sting of feeling like a failure and comparing himself to his relations drove him to succeed at any cost.

Cromwell and Winthrop shared another similarity: They were both only sons—in Cromwell's case, an only son who had seven sisters. When he was a teenager studying at Cambridge University—typical training for a boy of his age and background—his father died. Cromwell was apparently quite close to his mother, and although he married early, she lived in his household until her death, when he was fifty-five. As an adult, Cromwell gave in to destructive flashes of temper, and was often afflicted by emotional and physical diseases, until taking a decisive action propelled him out of his miseries. It may be that growing up in an overwhelmingly female household in an unusually intimate relationship with his mother was responsible for these character traits. Unfortunately, there is simply not enough evidence to know anything about his childhood development.

Cromwell grew up in an area of flat, marshy lands called the Fens. The modern novelist Graham Swift is from the same area, and he has written

about how that dull, gray, boggy landscape affects people born there: "However much you resist them, the waters will return; . . . the land sinks; silt collects; . . . something in nature wants to go back. . . . To live in the Fens is to receive strong doses of reality. The great, flat monotony of reality; the wide, empty space of reality. Melancholia and self-murder are not unknown in the

Oliver Cromwell's mother. (THE FOTOMAS INDEX)

Fens. Heavy drinking, madness, and sudden acts of violence are not uncommon."

Cromwell was given to periods of brooding that fit this pattern. In 1628 he visited a doctor, who diagnosed him as suffering from depression, which he called *valde melancholicus* (greatly sorrowful). One questionable source claims that in this same period he did nothing but lie in bed all day, fearing death and having strange visions of his future. Even if those details are dubious, the behavior sounds like him.

The most acute period of depression may have come not long after he visited the doctor, for his setbacks were mounting. In 1630 he lost out in a local political power struggle, sold his land, and moved to another town in the Fens. He was slipping down the social and economic scale, working in various local jobs to provide for his family. Like the wet marshland that resisted all efforts to drain it and make it productive, Oliver Cromwell and his family seemed to be sliding back into the muck.

And then something happened: Cromwell found God. Exactly as Winthrop experienced, reaching bottom led him to see the path that defined his life. As he wrote some years later to Oliver St. John, "You know what my manner of life has been. I was a chief, the chief of sinners. This is true; I hated godliness, yet God had a mercy on me. Oh the riches of His mercy! Praise Him for me, pray for me."

Does this confession mean that Cromwell was the notorious "town bull," who conducted many love affairs and fathered seven illegitimate children, as rumors later had it? Probably not. If anything, the language in his letter was rather standard; this was how many people who found God described their past. His words suggest that he was feeling trapped in his own limitations, weighed down by frustration and failure—and then something must have cut through the fog. He felt the healing touch of divine mercy. There was an alternative to the life he was leading, and that was to devote himself to God. Exactly like John Winthrop, he realized that he could not accomplish anything on his own, but that is exactly what allowed him to see beyond himself.

No wonder Cromwell felt that he did nothing by his own will but only in service to God. When he felt he knew God's wishes, he was the boldest, most forceful, most organized leader. When he did not, he was lost.

There is a strange parallel between what we can make out of Cromwell's inner life and that of King Charles. The king needed to be the unquestioned ruler, lest he slip back into being the sickly boy. Cromwell would be the agent of God or the brooding failure. Though no one would have predicted this when war broke out in earnest, the English Civil War turned out to be a contest between these two driven men.

Aside from the Bible, there was one book that shaped Cromwell's view of the world—Sir Walter Ralegh's *History of the World*. In describing historical events, Ralegh always searched for a deeper cause, which was divine judgment. He argued that "an omnipotent God visits upon sinful men and nations just and inevitable punishments." This was a belief Cromwell could agree with, and it was the only book he recommended for the education of his eldest son. But it was not just a lesson about the past. Ralegh had written the book while in the Tower of London as a kind of warning to King James, who had imprisoned him, and to educate his pupil and ally, Prince Henry. Now a man who took Ralegh's lessons to heart was preparing for war against the heir of King James, the disappointing replacement of Prince Henry. This was Cromwell's moment to be the avenging arm of divine judgment.

CAVALIER AND ROUNDHEAD

On August 22, 1642, King Charles I gathered his forces to do battle for his kingdom. His army would march beneath the royal standard, which read "Give Caesar His Due." This referred to the line in the Gospel according to Matthew, where Jesus explained that a believer must "render . . . unto Caesar the things which are Caesar's; and unto God the things that are God's" (Matthew 22:21). The banner suggested that Charles was owed obedience, while relations to God were another matter entirely.

His enemies had just the opposite belief. One popular book explained that Parliament's armies would have "the honor to execute the judgment that is written upon the Whore." They were not fighting their own rightful king but striving to destroy the Whore of Babylon—the vile creature described in Revelation chapter 17, which many Protestants took as a symbol of the Catholic Church.

Even though there were now two armies with about 20,000 soldiers apiece, this was not simply a case of king and nobles against gentry and commoners. There were nobles and commoners on both sides. Economic standing was not a good predictor of whom you would support. Many English people had divided loyalties. And even those who went to battle defined and redefined what they were fighting for as the war went on.

Still, each side quickly came up with a clear image of its enemy. To the forces of Parliament the king's men were "Cavaliers." The word is derived from the Spanish for *caballeros*—horse-riding nobility—and implied that these so-called Englishmen were all too high-flown, Spanish, and pro-Catholic. In turn, the royal forces sneered at their enemies as "Roundheads." William Prynne, whose index entry about the queen had cost him

This contemporary image is rare in that it makes fun of both sides, the long-haired Cavaliers and the well-cropped roundheads. (The Fotomas Index)

his ears, wrote about the "unloveliness of love-locks," criticizing fashionable long hair as impious. Because of strict religious views such as this, some early recruits did chop their hair off into the pageboy bowl cut.

The king's men came to be seen as loyal, romantic men of pride and breeding, who fought to the last even when their cause was lost. Sir John Suckling was one of the soldiers Charles had planned to employ to free the Earl of Strafford from prison. When that plot collapsed, he fled to Paris, where he committed suicide. He was also a poet and notorious seducer, both of which are evident in this typical Cavalier poem. It seems to be about war, but it is really about the pursuit of women:

A SOLDIER

I am a man of war and might
And know thus much, that I can fight,
Whether I am in the wrong or right,
　Devoutly.
No women under heaven I fear,
New oaths I can exactly swear,
And forty healths my brain will bear   [a "health" is a drinking toast]
　Most stoutly   [a pun on stout, a type of ale]
I cannot speak, but I can do
As much as any of our crew;
And if you doubt it, some of you
　May prove me.   ["prove" here means test]
I dare be bold thus much to say:
If that my bullets do but play   [implying, if we have sex]
You would be hurt so night and day,
　Yet love me.

Parliament's men were often seen as the opposite of everything in this poem: dour, disciplined, religious fanatics. In reality, the pro-Puritan poet Andrew Marvell wrote a very famous and seductive poem "To His Coy Mistress" that made as passionate an argument as possible that it is best not to wait, but to have sex right away, today. And Cromwell himself wore his hair as long as any Cavalier. In turn, there were devout Protestants who sided with the king.

Nonetheless, the contrasting images of Cavalier and Roundhead endured and even left their mark on American history. Many Union and

Confederate soldiers knew their English history quite well, and one great Civil War seemed to them very much like another. Diehard defenders of the Confederacy often identified with a previous generation of Cavaliers—romantic defenders of a lost cause—and it was easy to see the parallel between the industrious, devout, prim heirs of Winthrop and an earlier set of Puritans across the Atlantic.

"COME, MY BOYS, MY BRAVE BOYS"

The king's best chance to win the war came shortly after it began. Edgehill, the first battle of the war, was inconclusive. But because of bungling by Parliament's forces, the clash left Charles with a wide-open path to London. The leader of Parliament's men was the Earl of Essex, who was nothing at all like his commanding father. That Essex had been Ralegh's great rival, and was executed as a traitor after gambling his ambition against the heart of Queen Elizabeth I. His son was capable of his own dramatic acts—he brought his coffin with him into battle, as a kind of dare to fight to the end, but he was a mediocre general with none of his father's charisma.

Essex's greatest asset was his infantry, but after the battle of Edgehill his men began to desert. One young soldier, named Nehemiah Wharton, expressed some of the frustrations of the men in the field: "Our soldiers generally manifested our dislike of our Lieutenant-Colonel, who is a god-damn blade, and doubtless hatched in hell, and we all desire that either the Parliament would depose him or God convert him, or the Devil fetch him away." Essex's worst failing was that he had a habit of letting his enemy get between him and the place he was defending.

Bruno Ryves, a chaplain for King Charles, printed an ongoing account of the conflicts called Mercurius *Rusticus*. On the bottom of this page, which shows opening incidents of the Civil War, is a portrait of the battle of Edgehill. Parliament then began its own Mercurius to argue its point of view. Once again the political turmoil in England gave the press an opportunity to express a wide range of strong opinions, which was unheard of at the time.

Turnham
Green

Whitehall
Westminster

River Thames

St. Mary
the Virgin
Church

NORTH
SEA

ATLANTIC
OCEAN

Inverlochy

Aberdeen

Perth
Inveraray
Tippermuir
Glasgow
Dundee
Dunbar
Edinburgh
Berwick

Marston
Moor
York

Preston

Drogheda
Dublin

Leicester
Naseby

Huntingdon
Cambridge
Groton

Wexford

Edgehill

London

Bristol

Plymouth

ENGLAND, SCOTLAND, and IRELAND*
*With modern borders.

The king's nephew Prince Rupert was the royal General of the Horse. Trained in battle in Europe, he was an impassioned, at times brilliant, leader of the cavalry. His energy and courage seemed to give him a kind of divine—or diabolical—protection. Although he always plunged into the center of a battle with his spaniel, Boy, dashing around his horse's heels, he was never injured. With his long hair, good looks, winning self-confidence, and many love affairs, Rupert was the essence of the Cavalier. Pride, noble spirit, and contempt for his opponents were his guiding stars.

Rupert saw clearly what his uncle must do. Dash ahead, take London, arrest Pym and the other rebels, and be done with it. But Charles had other plans. He stopped to capture one town, paused to have a "triumphal entry" into Oxford, which he then used as his base of operations for the rest of the war, and waited for word from negotiators in London.

Charles's delays gave Essex time to reach London, and for the city to mobilize. Women as well as men dug trenches, preachers urged their congregations to prepare for battle, and 9,000 apprentices were given time off work to fight. They were joined by the city's own militia, its "trained bands." Rupert attacked first, on Saturday, November 12, 1642. Ten miles from the city he surprised a set of defenders, captured hundreds of prisoners, and plundered the town of Brentford. Among the prisoners was a captain named John Lilburne, who was later released in a prisoner exchange. His major part in English history was yet to come.

By the next morning, though, London was ready. "Come, my boys, my brave boys," urged Major General Philip Skippon, a leader of the Parliamentary forces. And come they did. The king's army woke to find itself facing 24,000 men on Turnham Green. Inspired by their preachers' Sunday sermons, the women of the city brought pies and meat, beer and wine to the hurriedly assembled troops. Faced with this show of strength,

Charles retreated. He would never come so close to taking London again.

Like the first Battle of Bull Run in the American Civil War, Turnham Green showed people that the war would not be over quickly, and England began to split apart into zones. The king and his supporters controlled a diagonal region that began at the Scottish border and slanted down and across the country, as well as a pocket in the extreme east. Parliament could count on associations of local commanders in an L-shaped territory to the north and east of London. The Eastern Association was led by the Earl of Manchester. One of the men under his command quickly found sixty horsemen to follow him. Captain Cromwell rushed off to engage his own band in as many local actions as he could. He was soon promoted to Colonel and given a horse regiment to lead.

Two horsemen decided the outcome of the war: Rupert and Cromwell. Each showed himself to be a fearless warrior and commanding leader, and they were both brilliant at using the most advanced military tool of their day, the organized cavalry charge. It took a year and a half for them to come face-to-face, and for much of that period the king held the advantage. His aim was still to capture London, and he had three armies in the field that made steady progress in that direction. In June 1643 the troublesome John Hampden was killed during a Parliamentary loss. In July Rupert took the port city of Bristol, the second largest city in the country. Holding a port gave the king access to arms and communications with his allies in Europe. The Earl of Newcastle was taking complete control of Yorkshire in the north.

Though the king did not know it, Parliament was being undermined by another loss. John Pym, the most able and determined leader of the opposition, was dying of cancer. He would not last out the year. But he was determined to accomplish one thing before he passed away: bring Scotland into the war again, this time as Parliament's full and open partner.

The Scots held out for one clear concession. They insisted that every man in both kingdoms join in a Solemn League and Covenant. This was a promise to adopt Presbyterianism. Should the joint armies prevail, the Scottish form of religion would rule over the entire island. Or at least that is what the Scots thought it said. Religious radicals in Parliament, who were going to war to resist the king's bishops, were no more eager to take direction from Scottish presbyters. Guided by Henry Vane Jr. they cleverly added a wiggle phrase to the covenant that left the whole matter open to reinterpretation.

Even as the king seemed to be winning within England, he faced a new threat to the north. But there was still another land he could call upon for support: Ireland. Charles had sent James Butler, the Duke of Ormonde, there to establish order. Now Butler and his army were recalled, giving Catholics control of much of Ireland and, in Ulster, the northern part of the island, leaving Protestants to battle for themselves. The challenge of the three kingdoms was no longer a puzzle, it was a series of interlocking wars.

Twenty-one thousand Scottish soldiers crossed into England in January 1644. Led by Alexander Leslie, they were a kind of holy band. Each regiment had a minister who led morning and evening prayers. Any soldier who swore or violated the Sabbath was punished. The army was not merely a conquering force but an example of the way of life it was fighting to enforce. The king knew he had to stop this invading army of believers, and he knew just where the battle would take place. His forces controlled the key northern city of York, which was directly in the path of the Scots. He must protect the city at all costs. But by summer Parliament's forces surrounded it. As Charles wrote to Rupert, "If York be lost I shall esteem my crown little less [than lost]." It was up to the fearless horseman to prevent that.

CHAPTER NINE

MARSTON MOOR

FORLORN HOPE

Parliament's generals knew that Rupert was coming, and they planned to intercept his men. But they reckoned without his energy and force of will. Setting off to the north when no one expected it, and pushing his troops to march twenty-two miles in a single day, Rupert did the impossible. He reached York unopposed and broke the siege of the city. Between Rupert's men and the legions of the Earl of Newcastle, the king now had a formidable force. But what should they do next?

Rupert was determined to strike out at once against Parliament's armies. York was not safe so long as the enemy was nearby. The prince also had direct instructions from the king to rush back to the south as soon as he could. Although Charles was not in immediate danger, there was no way to communicate that to his nephew in the north. The one way for Rupert to reach his king was by smashing through the lines of his enemies.

Parliament realized that this was their best chance to engage with Rupert and Newcastle. The Scots under Leslie were joined by Manchester's Eastern Association and by the Northern Army under Thomas Fairfax. On July 2, 1644, these five armies engaged in the largest battle ever fought in England; it decided the outcome of the Civil War.

As so often happens, the lay of the land defined the nature of the battle. The king's forces were arrayed on a flat plain called Marston Moor. This was perfect terrain for mounted horsemen. Whichever cavalry controlled the moor would likely win the day. Just in front of the king's men ran a long ditch, which divided the moor from nearby fields of grain. Rupert placed his horsemen near the ditch and in front of the moor, to prevent a frontal assault. For a good part of its length, the ditch was deep enough to be a formidable barrier, but on one flank it was quite shallow, making it all too easy to cross. Rupert lined this section with musketeers, who were now a living screen in front of the main army. That kind of manned trench was called a "forlorn hope," and the brave soldiers there had to take on the enemy charge alone, causing as much damage as they could before falling back.

Parliament's troops were forced to take their stand on the other side of the ditch amidst acres of annoying and frustrating growths. But they too had an advantage—their side of the field sloped up slightly to Marston Hill. The highest point, just one hundred feet up, is a knoll known to this day as Cromwell's Plump. Riding down this slope gave Parliament's riders a bit of extra speed as they charged into battle.

It took much of the day for both sides to get their forces into the field and in the right positions. Across the ditch, they were just four hundred

This contemporary painting of Prince Rupert by Gerrit van Honthorst captures his aristocratic manner. His expression suggests both refinement and contempt. (NATIONAL PORTRAIT GALLERY, LONDON)

yards apart, with Rupert's cavalry lined up directly in the path of Cromwell's. Though all were in place by four in the afternoon, a strange calm descended an hour later. The devout Protestants on Parliament's side began singing psalms, and the king's men were close enough to hear them. Time now became an enemy. The 18,000 men with perhaps 5,000 horses on the king's side and the 25,000 or so men with 5,000 horses for Parliament were staring at each other, feeling the seconds pass, knowing Hell was about to open up all around them but not knowing when.

By seven Rupert decided that it was too late to fight. "We will charge them tomorrow morning," he announced. As he retreated to eat, the skies turned ominously dark, as if to insist that this was the appointed hour for a battle. Great thunder clashes followed, and the troops were pelted with summer hail. Just as the frozen water fell from the sky, the three allied armies surged down the slope and into battle.

The initial charge amid the storm looked to one observer as if the black clouds themselves were rolling down the hills. The attacking soldiers could barely see or hear, the combat "made such a noise with shot and clamor of shouts that we lost our ears, and the smoke of powder was so thick that we saw no light but what proceeded from the mouths of guns."

Scottish dragoons—mounted foot soldiers—beat a path across the ditch, and Cromwell's cavalry charged ahead. They did not gallop helter-skelter. Instead, they moved together as one, keeping a tight rein on their horses. With their exquisite control, the men could ride so close to each other that one knee practically touched another. "We came down the hill in the bravest order," recalled a cavalry leader, "and with the greatest resolution that ever was seen. . . . In a moment we were past the ditch into the moor, upon equal grounds with the enemy, our men going in a running march." *First blood to Parliament.*

As soon as Rupert realized that the fighting had begun, he rushed into battle. The prince accosted fleeing men and rallied them to return to the fight. Newly energized, Rupert's forces stopped Cromwell's men in their tracks, and it is likely that Cromwell himself was slashed with a sword and had to leave the field for a short while to be bandaged. It took an attack from Scottish forces coming from the other direction to free Cromwell's cavalry. *Counter to the king, but Parliament still has momentum.*

All this action was on one wing of the battlefield. On the other a bad situation for Parliament was turning into a disaster. Fairfax had much trouble

getting across the ditch, and when he did, his forces splintered. Some horsemen broke through the enemy line and stormed ahead, others were trapped
in hard fighting; meanwhile, the king's men poured across in the other direction and routed Fairfax's rear troops. The Royalists galloped on, ransacking
the now unprotected supplies Fairfax had left behind and causing panic
among the many spectators who had come to watch. *Second front, advantage
to the king.*

With armies charging through each other, there was chaos and misery
everywhere, and no clear line between the forces. One Royalist later recalled

Opposing forces, battle of Marston Moor.

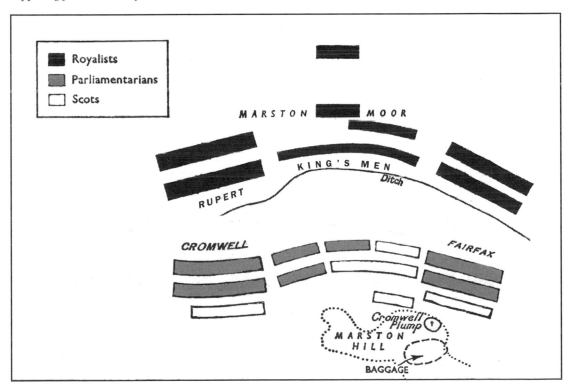

that "in the fire, smoke and confusion of that day I knew not for my soul whither to incline [where to go]. The runaways on both sides were so many, so breathless, so speechless, so full of fears, that I should not have taken them for men." A section of Scots, he reported, ran past him crying, "Wae's [woe is] us, we are all undone."

They very nearly were, for the king's army was close to routing one whole side of Parliament's army, which would have given the Royalists a clear victory. Another group of Scots, though, fought grimly on. They jammed their sixteen-foot pikes into the ground, knelt down next to these wooden lances, and resisted charge after charge. This brave stand bought time. Then Fairfax himself tried a bold gambit.

There was no single uniform for either army. Instead, each company within an army had its own colors, which it might display on a standard. In the first battles Royalists often wore crimson silk scarves, while the Parliamentary forces favored orange, but this was no sure means of identifying friend or foe. At Marston Moor, Parliamentary soldiers identified themselves with field signs—little white bands or even pieces of paper stuck into their caps. Fairfax removed his field sign and dashed through enemy lines unrecognized, searching for someone to bring help to his embattled troops.

IRONSIDES

Fairfax, or perhaps another horseman, reached Cromwell. Most cavalry leaders tended to charge straight ahead once they had broken the enemy. Rupert's men, for example, went into battle at a gallop, hoping to sweep all before them. Triumphant horsemen would then ride miles away from the battle to plunder baggage trains. Cromwell had learned a lesson in one of his earliest battles. Instead of allowing his horsemen to rampage ahead after their initial victory, he kept them under his strict and exacting control. That allowed him to bring them back into the fray.

At Marston Moor the armies had switched sides, which put the most successful Royalist forces just where their opponents had been a few hours before. Cromwell regrouped his men on the moor and led them back across the ditch in the opposite direction to attack the rear of the soldiers who had scattered Fairfax's men.

By now a bright moon lit the bloody battlefield. Cromwell's horsemen had won the first round in their initial attack, and they carried the day in the end, smashing through the king's troops just when the Royalists thought they were on the verge of triumph. The victorious army knelt together, sang a psalm in celebration of victory, and settled down to rest. *Cromwell wins the battle.*

The brave and dashing Rupert had forced the battle of Marston Moor to begin, but the disciplined Cromwell brought it to its end. Rupert realized he had been beaten by Cromwell and gave him the nickname Ironside. In time, Cromwell's cavalry came to be called Ironsides. Their close-order riding, almost breastplate to breastplate, made them a kind of ironclad unit, a united force no individual riders could resist.

These disciplined horsemen were not just a product of the endless drill most cavalry commanders used to turn their men into elegant, well-trained riders. Cromwell's riders respected and admired him, and he, in turn, treated them well. He enjoyed joking and talking with his men as equals. He constantly took their part, haranguing Parliament to get them their pay and

Englands Miraculous Preservation Emblematically Described, Erected
for a perpetuall MONVMENT to Posterity.

Earle of Essex   Earle of Warwick   Earle of Manchester   Generall Lesley

Though Englands Ark haue furies storms jndur'd
By Plotts of foes and power of the sword
Yet to this day by Gods almighty hand
The Ark's preserud and almost safe at land

House of Lords   House of Comons   Assembly

Sr Tho: Fairfax   Leif: Gen: Cromwell

THis Ark cal'd Union hath not her Peer
On Earth, & 's laden with a fraught so dear
To her Almighty Pilo', that no waves
Of might or malice rais'd b' infernal slaves
Of human shape and lofty high estate,
Nor yet their father that inveterate
Old Serpent raging 'gainst this blessd Bark
The Antitype of righteous Noahs Ark
Can make to sink or split upon the rocks
Of ruine, maugre all their furious knocks
Of powdered bals, and force of armed steel
By violence to make this Ark to feel
Their wrathful open rage, when neither plots
Nor treacheries fast tyed with the knots
Of vows, and Sacraments of miracles,
Impostures, fascinations, and spels,
Espoused interests of Potentates
Forraign and home-bred Soldiers, and Prelates;
Threats, Promises, and Protestations,
Aulick Libels, Lyes, and Defamations,
Nor all the cunning, study, pains, and sweat
Of all Malignant Foxes smal, and great;
In Court, and Campe, City, and Countrie,
Nor in this Ark (if any lurking lie)
Can break this Churches Trinity of State
Described here, nor make them violate
That pious Covenant, which hol's them fast,
And is indeed that Vessels mainest Mast,
By which she saileth through the troubled seas
Of her affairs; and now hath found some ease,
Thanks be unto that heavenly Cynosure
Above the Stars, which gives a light t' allure
Her Mariners, and yet wil give light more
T' unfold the secrets of the Romish Who e,
The hellish darknefs of those mists and fogs
Of blasphemies, and errors, which those froggs
Or unclean Spirits from the Beast proceeding,
(whose thoughts upon Reformers blood are feeding)
Have now unbowelled, and spread about
To put the light of Reformation out,
And with new Hydra-headed heresies
(Like to that smoke ; t' obscure the clearest skies
Of sacred Truth (a devillish designe
More dangerous, then was the Powder-Myne)

And raise tempestuous storms about this Ark,
And now they cannot beat by force, they bark
Belch, and disgorge their Stygian despight
'Gainst the Protector of this Ark outright;
And stil their horrid rage doth more abound
Because this Ark of Union is not drown'd;
But wait a while, and see this cursed crew
Pertake of that reward, that's here in view:
For fix your eyes upon these Seas of ire
Involving those, that did 'gainst th' Ark conspire:
See here some headlesse floating in the waves
Of direful death, some dead, and wanting graves:
See all their warlike Engines, and their Forces,
Now as feeble as their livelefs Corfes;
See these bloody men and their Commission
To kil Innocents brought to perdition;
And they that living yet thoug't it no sin
To leave this Ark, now with they had kept in;
But now they are the scorn of time, and fate,
Who did this tossed Bark despise, and hate,
Augmented more in that they did remove
The Royal Steers-man, whom our Ark doth love.
But see these noble Champions (lately fix)
Guarding th' assaulted Union, and fix
Themselves to courage, valor, care, and love
To bring to rest this tossed Turtle-dove.
Their brave atchievements Chronicles shal speak,
And learned Volumes; but my pen's too weak
To tel their worth, or their due praises spread,
Whom great JEHOVAH hath so honor'd.
Draw neer, kind Reader, do but view this peece,
'Tis not of Jason, nor of his Golden fleece
That here is Emblem'd, nor the high renown
Of Hectors Acts ere Troy was batter'd down,
That here we shew you, but it doth presage
A warry Landskip of a weeping Age.
The Ark that rideth here whole tender wals
Contains in her our English Admirals,
For Reformation swimming on the Main,
'Gainst Superstition which so much di'd raign:
Charge on, charge on, the guard of Pluto al,
The Pope, the Bishop, and the Cardinal:
But you had best retire, 'tis all but vain,
For truth hath gotten higher, and she wil raign.

Here Reader pause, and judge our Land is free,
A Chronicle for our posterite;
For Goshath brought them, so their pride doth swage
And we made happy in a peaceful Age.
Had not the LORD bin for us, they had won,
And cloth'd this Land with red confusion;
But now sail on you worthies through the Ocean
Of sad distempers, let your winged Motion
Out pace the flight of Eagles, that aspire
Go take your Senfers fil'd with zealous fire:
Let truth comand the way, by her the Ark is guided,
And let the Gospel sway, and Errors be avoyded:
Great Godot wind & sea, who searcheth thro' the dark
Who didst command old Noah to enter in the Ark,
Direct this ARK unto the Key of peace,
Command deliverance that our Wars may cease.

An Apostrophe to the Church.

THen woman thou whose clothing is the Sun,
Cease to complain, nor say thou art undone,
For thou hast suffered harder things of yore,
Than now; weigh with the present times before.
Seest thou not how thy sad and heavy night
Of fears and forrows now are vanisht quite:
Triumphing days thy late griefs do beguile,
And Halcyon times begin again to smile.
Behold how rugged Mars is posting hence,
Seeing thee armed so with heav'n defence:
Outward enmitie shal not hurt a jot,
If thine intestine Errors hurt thee not.
Then wipe thy blubbered face, and lay aside
Thy mourning weeds, and like a loving Bride
With spirit mounted on a heavenly flame
Spread abroad thy Bridegrooms glorious fame;
What tongue of mortal, men or Seraphim
Can tel sufficiently the praise of him.

By John Leicester.

LONDON, Printed for John Hancock, and are to be sold at his shop, at the entrance into Popes head Ally. 1646.

to give them better clothing and equipment. Most of all, though, he cared for his men no matter who they were, or even how they prayed.

Fighting against the forces of royalty, of birth and blood, Oliver Cromwell had a very different sense of how to evaluate a man, and a soldier: "I would rather have a plain russet-coated captain that knows what he fights for, and loves what he knows, than that which you call 'a gentleman' and is nothing else. I honor a gentleman that is so indeed." While Cromwell would have preferred to use trained gentlemen in his service, he was able to see past the prejudices of his day and recognize the ability of the men who actually rallied to his cause. He forged a great fighting unit by taking the bold step of putting the man ahead of his lineage.

But his fellow commanders were not happy about this. The Earl of Manchester, leader of Parliament's armies, for example, complained that "Colonel Cromwell's raising of his regiment makes choice of his officers not such as were soldiers or men of estate, but such as were common men, poor and of mean parentage." Denzil Holles, a conservative Parliamentary leader, claimed that "most of the colonels are tradesmen, brewers, tailors, goldsmiths, shoemakers and the like." This was not meant as a compliment to the democracy of the troops but rather a condemnation of their obvious lack of good breeding and social standing.

While the English Civil War did not begin as a social revolution, something new was taking place in battle. The greatest commander on the field understood that the enemy was not merely the forces of the king; it was a

Opposite: *In this drawing, many of the key leaders of Parliament's forces are shown surrounding England's embattled ship of state. England is like Noah's ark, carrying the faithful, while Charles raises his sword from water trying to destroy it.*　(THE FOTOMAS INDEX)

rigid, hierarchical way of looking at the world that hid an individual's talents behind his rank.

Cromwell was concerned about his men's spiritual state, and he wanted "honest, sober Christians" in his ranks. But here too the experience of serving next to brave men of conscience led him to a new and unexpected conclusion. "The state," he argued, "in choosing men to serve them, takes no notice of their opinions; if they be willing faithfully to serve them, that satisfies." In other words, a good soldier was a good soldier, no matter what he believed in. Bloody combat led Oliver Cromwell to the very same opinion his friend Roger Williams had arrived at through the relentless search for spiritual perfection—the belief in religious toleration.

Cromwell, a devout Puritan, fighting for a Parliament that had solemnly vowed to turn England into a Presbyterian country, was now advocating acceptance of more than one brand of Protantism. As he later put it in a famous, impassioned letter objecting to the Scots' desire to impose religious uniformity, "I beseech you, in the bowels of Christ, think it possible that you may be mistaken."

In time, urged by Williams, Cromwell would even take the lead in permitting Jews to return to England, from which they had been banned since 1290. Though he continued to have hesitations about Catholics, with their supposed allegiance to the Pope and complicity in what he believed were horrible Irish massacres, he became a spokesman for a limited kind of "liberty of conscience." Once again, Manchester did not like this development. He saw Cromwell's men as a group of unhinged fanatics: "If you look upon his own regiment of horse, see what a swarm there is of those that call themselves the godly; some of them profess they have seen visions and had revelations."

The conflict over how to build Heaven on Earth was bringing unexpected results. In England, Oliver Cromwell argued for religious tolerance and seemed to accept inspired soldiers as long as they followed orders. In New England, John Winthrop exiled Williams for his beliefs and Hutchinson for her revelations. Told of the trend toward tolerance in England, Winthrop grumbled that once they saw "a little more of the lawlessness of liberty of conscience they will change their judgments."

The New England Puritans could, for the moment, enforce their vision of religious perfection. But their opponents could always move on to other places to create their own settlements. The America that the Puritans helped to found would be a place in which an endless variety of religions and immigrant communities could establish their own rules, but people were constantly on the move, seeking new answers. Even within New England the Puritans adopted a new church structure called Congregationalism. Unlike both Episcopalians and Presbyterians, Congregationalists believe that, within well-defined limits, each congregation and pastor can work out its own version of Protestantism. The Civil War in England bought time for the New England Puritans. As long as the king was preoccupied, they were free to develop their own brand of severe Protestantism. But eventually the war would end, and whatever decisions were made on religion in England were sure to cross the Atlantic. The Puritans could be intolerant only as long as London tolerated them.

Older history books claim that religious toleration was a founding theme of America. It would be more accurate to say that religious toleration was an idea that arose from the same forces that led to the creation of some of the American colonies. Yet it was an idea the leaders of those same colonies did their best to reject.

CHAPTER TEN

THE NEW MODEL

CALCULATING GENERAL OR GODLY SERVANT?

After the battle of Marston Moor, Cromwell's brilliant command gave Parliamentary forces a good chance of winning the war. Yet the sudden rise of this soldier with the strange ideas made Parliament very nervous. What, after all, was Parliament's goal? To please the Scots by enforcing the Solemn League and Covenant? The Puritans hated this idea. To force the king to be less arrogant and more cooperative? Soldiers who believed that they were fighting a holy war did not want to die just to wrest more promises from an untrustworthy king. But the majority of Parliament were sober men who would rather have a tamer king and a Presbyterian nation than Cromwell and chaos.

Though the Scots and Parliamentary Presbyterians appreciated Cromwell as a commander, they saw him as an increasingly dangerous leader. Rumor had it that Cromwell "hoped to live to see never a noble-man in England." This was not true, but it indicates what a frightening fig-ure he had become: a popular, confident military leader, who seemed comfortable with the most radical elements in the land. The Presbyterians were eager to make peace with the king and to stop the spread of fanatical religion and social ferment. Cromwell was their living nightmare.

The army and its supporters in Parliament followed Cromwell in insist-ing that most varieties of Protestantism should be tolerated. This did not mean they were any less convinced that there was one truth, one way to God. They thought that time and God would bring all of the saved to the right way. Fallible humans should not try to impose a single top-down rule. Instead, earnest Protestant seekers should be permitted to pursue their own paths, their own pilgrimages to that truth. Termed the Independents, they believed they were doing God's work in holy combat, and they were dead set against a peace settlement until they achieved complete victory. Cromwell was their hero.

The split of Presbyterians and Independents, advocates of peace and of war, was further complicated because Parliament was ultimately responsible for the war effort. Legislators were generals, and commanders served in Parliament. As a result, politics interfered with military planning. At the same time, politicians didn't like being pressured by the popularity of sol-diers. On December 9, 1644, Cromwell proposed a novel solution to this leadership tangle. According to his Self-Denying Ordinance, all members of Parliament would have to resign their posts as military commanders. This would ensure that the Earl of Manchester, who Cromwell thought was dragging his heels on the battlefield, would be replaced. But it would also remove Cromwell, the man conservative legislators most feared, from his soldiers. Cromwell assured Parliament that his resignation would not create any problems, for his men "do not idolize me, but look upon the cause they fight for."

With the established leaders and their contending agendas bowing out, Parliament had the opportunity to blend their forces together and build a new, more unified, and stronger army. The army was, in their words, "new modeled." As a sign of its new nature, all the infantry adopted the uniform that had become common in the Eastern Association, a red coat. This remained the official color of the British army for the next 250 years. Ironically, the red coat, which in American history came to symbolize the forces of the king fighting against George Washington and democracy, began as the emblem of Cromwell and Parliament battling against Charles I.

Cromwell urged that Fairfax be named Commander in Chief, and he was. Skippon, who had rallied London's apprentices at Turnham Green, was put in charge of the infantry. But who would replace Cromwell? Delay followed delay as Parliament decided what to do, and Cromwell hesitated to send in his resignation. By June 1645 Fairfax himself requested that his best cavalry leader be appointed Lieutenant General of the Horse and second in command of the army as a whole.

How did this happen? How could Cromwell support a bill designed specifically to get him out of the army, only to wind up as the second in command of the New Model Army? Was he a cynical calculator, a general on the rise who was stirring up revolutionary sentiment while manipulating his way to take control of England? Precisely this pattern has been used by many military leaders turned dictators throughout world history.

Or, as he claimed, was he actually willing to resign, and continued to serve only because he was asked to and believed that he was doing God's will? Though this sounds so odd to modern ears as to be unbelievable, it is plausible, and there is simply not enough historical evidence to decide the matter. Cromwell's backers in Parliament wanted him to keep fighting, so the choice was not his alone. But whether he engineered the whole resignation scheme to eliminate his opponents and clear the path to his own ambition remains one of the central questions in understanding his life.

NASEBY

However Cromwell came to be in the field in June 1645, it was most fortunate for Parliament that he did. In Scotland the Marquis of Montrose, with an army he had pieced together out of Scots-Irish soldiers returning home and Scottish highlanders, stormed into battle on behalf of his king. Fighting close to home, the kilt-clad soldiers disappeared after each battle, but they achieved one amazing victory after another. They took Perth, defeated a large force at Tippermuir, routed David Lord Elcho—whose troops had been told that the Holy Ghost assured their victories—and captured Aberdeen. They joined with the Maclean and Macdonald clans to slaughter the Campbells and burn Inveraray. Flushed with success, Montrose invited the king to come north and win the war from there. He then went on to take Inverlochy, capture Dundee, and win the capital city of Glasgow itself.

Montrose's victories split Parliament's forces. Their Scots allies wanted to return home to deal with him, and they increasingly demanded that the New Model Army fight for itself. As Parliament wrangled, Rupert marched. By the end of May he was ready to attack Leicester, a wealthy town that strongly supported Parliament. He demanded its surrender, and when the town fathers sent out a trumpeter with a mission to request a night to decide on what to do, he gave them fifteen minutes.

When the city resisted, Rupert's siege turned into a slaughter. His horsemen "scoured the town," showing little mercy and murdering women as well as the many Scots they found fighting against them. "Scarse a cottage" was left "unplundered." This was the New Model Army's first test, and it was a disaster.

Even though mapping England had been one of the accomplishments of Sir Walter Ralegh's day, when armies were fighting far from their home territories, commanders on both sides still had only limited knowledge of where they were. There simply were no detailed local maps, and there was poor intelligence. The two armies lost touch with each other, met up by accident, and then hurriedly had to decide where to fight on the unfamiliar terrain. As troops circled near Leicester, the king faced a second problem. One of his generals inexplicably stalled, failing to bring his 3,000 mounted soldiers. Even Rupert, who always leapt into battle, thought this was not the time to fight. But Charles and his other top advisers were contemptuous of the New Model Army and would not listen.

By June 13 the two armies half planned, half stumbled into each other's path near the village of Naseby; the battle would come the next day. Once again the two sides lined up as they had on Marston Moor, with mounted forces on both wings and infantry in the center. Rupert's cavalry faced a

Opposite: *Two nineteenth-century depictions of soldiers in the Civil War. The dashing long-haired cavalier bears a resemblance to the Three Musketeers as they are often depicted in movies—which makes sense, since that novel is set in 1625 and concerns the French side of the same Protestant and Catholic conflicts that led up to the Civil War in England. The New Model Army soldiers correctly wear shoes, not boots, and menacing but functional helmets.*   (BOTH IMAGES THE FOTOMAS INDEX)

group that had just been put under the command of Henry Ireton, an intelligent, articulate Puritan leader, who was soon to marry one of Cromwell's daughters. On the other wing Cromwell's three rows of Ironsides were opposed by only two rows under the leadership of Sir Marmaduke Langdale. Lacking the 3,000 men who had never arrived, the king had about 4,500 mounted men, 2,000 fewer than his enemy. Cromwell was overjoyed, for he knew just what this meant. As he later wrote, "I could not . . . but smile out to God in praises, in assurance of victory."

Rupert, being Rupert, had to attack first, and at ten in the morning he did. He and his brother Maurice charged into troops led by the inexperienced Ireton and, despite being outnumbered, swept through them. Such rapid success was perhaps the worst thing that could have happened to them, for Rupert's Cavaliers simply kept on riding and riding, until they reached Fairfax's baggage train. There they met determined soldiers, who fought back and preoccupied them for the rest of the battle.

The royal infantry also showed its strength, for despite being outnumbered nearly two to one, it dominated the middle. But no matter how well the king's forces were doing, there was always Cromwell. His horsemen charged ahead in their perfect jog trot and sent Langdale's horsemen racing for their lives. The new lieutenant general showed his cool brilliance, for Cromwell split his forces, sending one group methodically to hunt down the fleeing enemy and turning the others back into the battle. Just as at Marston Moor, he was able to swing his disciplined riders around to attack again. With Rupert pinned down in combat a mile from the battle, and Cromwell's Ironsides calmly returning to it, the royal infantry was trapped. They had no cavalry to protect them.

Though Rupert eventually reached the field and tried to organize a last stand, the battle was over, and he and Charles had to flee for their lives. The

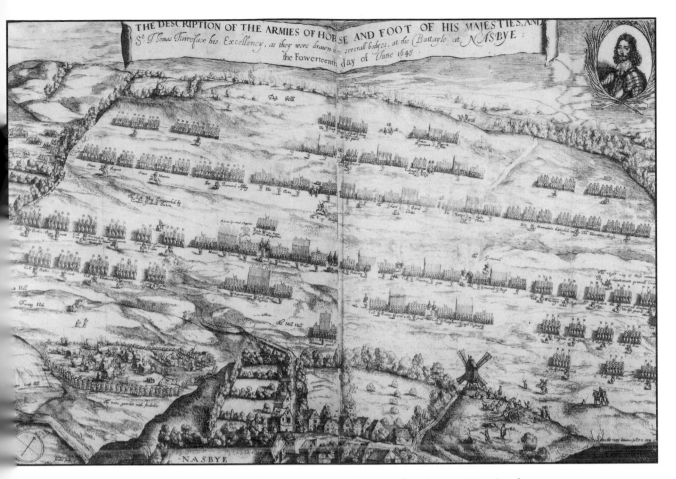

Robert Streeter made this engraving of the battle lines at the start of the battle of Naseby about a year after it took place; it is thought to be generally accurate. Cromwell's forces are on the far right bottom, facing off against Langdale. Rupert is speeding on horseback in front of his men on the left, near his brother Maurice, and paired against Ireton's men. (THE FOTOMAS INDEX)

battle was not merely a loss for the king, it was a disaster. Forty-five hundred of his soldiers surrendered. He lost thousands of guns, and that was not the worst of it. Searching through the king's captured baggage, Parliament's soldiers found two years of his correspondence with his wife. This revealed secret plots to bring over an army of Irish Catholics and to hire foreign soldiers. The king's own letters proved him to be the very worst conspirator the Puritans could have imagined.

Parliament's troops showed their own brand of religious passion when they came upon a large group of camp followers—women attached to soldiers, either as wives or prostitutes. Many of the women were Welsh and did not speak English, but the soldiers thought this meant they were Irish, the most hated of enemies. The soldiers executed at least 100; many others were slashed—a sign that they were thought to be prostitutes.

Cromwell shared this fear and hatred of Catholicism, and especially of Irish Catholics, though he was not part of the attack on the women. Instead, he took his first free moment on the battlefield to make a plea to Parliament for his own brand of religious toleration: "Honest men served you faithfully in this action. Sir, they are trusty. I beseech you in the name of God not to discourage them. I wish this action may beget thankfulness and humility in all that are concerned in it. He that ventures his life for the liberty of his country, I wish he trust God for the liberty of his conscience, and you for the liberty he fights for."

After Naseby the fighting on the battlefield was essentially over. There was no chance that Charles could win by force of arms. But that did not mean the war had come to an end. Even as one after another of the king's strongholds surrendered, England grew ever more divided. And Charles knew that his best chance was to keep playing one faction against the other, until all agreed with him that there could be no peace until he was returned to rule.

What was the British Heaven, how could the English live well in the sight of God? What should the relationship among ruler, legislators, and people be? Warfare pushed people in two opposite directions: toward the kind of battle-hardened ferocity that resulted in massacres of women by Royalists in Leicester and by Parliament's men after Naseby, or toward at least a limited form of religious toleration. After the war new questions began to arise. Perhaps the key to Heaven was not in perfect faith after all. Perhaps it would not come until people lived in a perfected society.

MURDER BY PRAYER

Across the ocean, in New England, Cromwell's triumphs brought an equally troubling set of questions. Stephen Marshall, the English preacher whose stirring sermons encouraged Parliament to take up arms against the king, had quoted a famous passage, Judges 5:23, that cursed those who "came not to the help of the Lord . . . against the mighty." He meant the Puritans in New England. John Cotton in Boston understood the criticisms so well that he almost seemed to agree while trying to deny them. "It is a serious misrepresentation," he argued in 1648, "to say that our brethren . . . fled from England like mice from a crumbling house, anticipating its ruin, prudently looking to their own safety, and treacherously giving up the defense of the common cause of the Reformation." Cotton had reassured the godly that America was a Land of Promise, set aside for them by God. Now the best he could do was to protest that it was not entirely an escape hatch for cowards. In fact, many of the faithful who had come over in the Great Migration had been fleeing from Archbishop Laud and King Charles. Now that the fight for England was blazing, where should they be? Where did God want his faithful to assemble in preparation for the final days? Ironically, the very success of the Parliamentary forces in England was a challenge to New England's reason for being.

Some New Englanders returned to England to fight in the Civil War. Ten reached the rank of major or higher in Parliament's armies, while oth-

John Leverett (1616–1679) arrived in Boston with his parents in 1633. When he returned to England in 1644 to fight against the king's armies, he wore this ox-hide coat. "Buff coats" like this were worn beneath breastplates. They were thick enough to protect soldiers but not as heavy as full armor. Leverett returned to Massachusetts in 1648 and served as governor from 1672 to 1679.
(COURTESY MASSACHUSETTS HISTORICAL SOCIETY, IMAGE 422)

ers went home to preach or to be elected as members of Parliament. Vane was appointed as Treasurer. The Great Migration of Puritans to the New World ended and even began to run in reverse. Those who stayed were left with the challenge of explaining why—where did New England figure in God's plans, if the final battles against the Antichrist were taking place in England? One answer was prayer. In regular services and on special fast days, congregations were asked to launch their invisible artillery against the Royalist forces. A preacher named William Hooke explained that the colonists must "lie in wait in the wilderness, to come upon the backs of God's enemies with deadly fasting and prayer, murderers that will kill point blank from one end of the world to another."

Through their prayers, the New England Puritans could feel they were participating in the battles, contributing to the victories. Some even began to think of Cromwell as the Messiah, the divine leader. Then, as Presbyterians, Independents, Scots, and the king wrangled over England's future, New England's leaders decided that they had yet another role to play. God had kept them out of the battles so that they could develop a new form of Protestantism midway between the forms of the Presbyterians and the Independents. The New England Way, as they called it, or Congregationalism, as it is termed today, was there as a model to save the homeland.

In England, though, the crisis about the future of the country was taking a new turn. Arguments about God were shifting to clashes over society and government. And these raging debates would, in time, make their way across the Atlantic. When they did, the Land of Promise would come to have an entirely new meaning.

HEAVEN
OR HELL?

CHAPTER ELEVEN

AGREEMENT OF THE PEOPLE

"HIGH AND VERY GREAT CONTENTIONS"

"Every man that is to live under a government ought first by his own consent, to put himself under that government." *Every man*—not just men of wealth, not just men of proud birth, not just those who share the faith supported by the government. *His own consent*—government is an agreement, not a fact of birth, or an obligation to an overlord whom it is our humble duty to serve. These ideas were revolutionary when Abraham Lincoln rephrased them as "government of the people, by the people, and for the people" in 1863; still more so in 1789 when James Madison wrote in the United States Constitution that "we the people" had settled upon a way to form a "more perfect Union"; they caused a war in 1776 when Thomas Jefferson declared that the colonists had "unalienable rights" to "life, liberty, and the pursuit of happiness."

The idea that government is an agreement between the people and the politicians that limits the power of both is the foundation of American democracy. But the sentence at the beginning of this chapter was not crafted in the nineteenth century or the eighteenth. It did not come from any of the well-known Founding Fathers of the United States. Instead, it was spoken by a member of the English army in October 1647. He and his fellow radicals dared to propose ideas that were more than a century ahead of their time. Colonel Thomas Rainborough arrived at these shocking ideas in the furious debates that began once the first phase of the war against Charles was over.

All wars bring unexpected results. The English Civil War acted as a crucible. People, causes, and beliefs were hurled against each other with such force that old ways of seeing the world were shattered, and radicals began to entertain ideas of liberty and democracy that had never before been expressed. But it took the failure of peace for these ideas to be spoken in public.

As the New Model Army completed its conquests, Charles scrambled to seek safety. He escaped to Scotland, hoping to make a deal with the very people whose resistance to his prayer book had set in motion the war he had just lost. While the Scots were willing to talk, their goal remained the same—making Presbyterianism the faith of all the British Isles. Charles could not agree, and by the end of 1646 the Scots decided to sell him to Parliament for a ransom of £400,000. On January 30, 1647, the king was returned to England as a prisoner of his enemies. Parliament was in a strong position. It had bought off the Scots, and now it held the king. It had just one more force to bring under its control: the army.

Parliament's Presbyterian majority was eager to disband the army and reluctant to pay the soldiers their wages, honor them for their victories, or listen to pleas—even from Cromwell himself—for religious toleration. The Presbyterians saw the New Model Army in much the same way as many southern whites viewed black soldiers after World Wars I and II: dangerous men who had learned to fight and kill and might no longer be willing to accept their humble roles. In the New Model Army not only were common men armed and trained, but they had proved themselves to be the best soldiers in England. If they were not quickly disbanded and returned to their homes, who knew what changes in English life they might demand? And yet Parliament needed to hold on to some soldiers in order to retake Ireland, where the hated Catholics, some actively supported by the Pope, were in control.

Led by Cromwell, many soldiers had come to feel that they were acting out God's own plans in battle. That is why they would always win, no matter whom they faced. Inspired fighters under divine guidance were not about to accept being treated as hired guns whose term was up; they demanded to be heard.

An otherwise unknown man named James Pitson was compelled to publish a pamphlet expressing his views. "I beseech your honors to pardon my boldness in writing, but I have waited these two years for my money out of purse, and have spent as much in waiting as the money is worth and have nothing to live on these twelve months whereby to maintain myself and my family but what I have borrowed, and am now speedily to go to Ireland and have nothing to leave my family in my absence."

Pitson spoke urgently and humbly. Others were more angry. Some of these disaffected men came to be called Levellers, a negative term used much the way twentieth-century critics spoke of Communists—dangerous extremists who wanted to remove all distinctions between people. The frustrated soldiers also began to elect spokesmen, whom they called Agitators, or agents, to express their grievances.

Cromwell, Fairfax, and Ireton were in the middle. They were attentive to the army and sympathetic to its frustrations, but loyal to Parliament and determined to keep order. As Cromwell told a gathering of vocal, angry officers, if "authority falls to nothing, nothing can follow but confusion." The more restless, angry, and demanding the army grew, the more determined Parliament was to disband it quickly. Presbyterian legislators began to consider making alliances with the Scots, or even the king, to overmatch their own army. In turn, the Independents in Parliament and in the army tested out making new deals with the king that would give them the upper hand over the Presbyterians. This was a perfect position for Charles, as Fairfax realized. The king was now "the Golden Ball cast between the two parties."

But balls, even golden ones, do not decide where they will land, and on June 3, 1647, an army officer named George Joyce, backed by two units of mounted men, seized the king. The odds now shifted—the army had the king, and it no longer trusted Parliament. "We are not a mere mercenary army hired to serve any arbitrary power of a state," they protested. If the army was not merely the obedient arm of Parliament, it needed to have a program of its own. But what would that be?

Cromwell and Fairfax met with Charles to see if they could work out an agreement on England's future—and seriously considered a proposal that included toleration for Catholics. But Levellers and Agitators insisted that they, too, have a voice in determining which British Heaven would emerge out of the ruins of war.

THE CHRISTIAN MANS TRIALL:
OR,
A TRVE RELATION
of the first apprehension and severall ex-
aminations of *IOHN LILBVRNE*,

With his Cenfure in *Star-Chamber*, and the manner
of his cruell whipping through the Streets : where-
unto is annexed his Speech in the Pillory, and
their gagging of him:

Alfo the fevere Order of the Lords made the fame day for
fettering his hands and feet in yrons, and for keeping his friends
and monies from him, which was accordingly executed upon
him for a long time together by the Wardens of the *Fleet*, with
a great deale of barbarous cruelty and inhumanity, &c.

Revel. 2.10. *Behold, the Divell fhall caft fome of you into prifon, that you may
be tryed, and youfhall have tribulation ten dayes : be thou faithfull unto death, and I
will give thee a Crowne of life.*
Matth. 10. 19. *But when they deliver you up, take no thought how, or what you
fhall fpeake, for it fhall be given you in that howre what you fhall fay.*

The fecond Edition, with an addition.

LONDON,
Printed for **WILLIAM LARNAR**, and are to be fold at
his Shop at the Signe of the *Golden Anchor*, neere
Pauls-Chaine, 1 6 4 1.

Gaze not vpon this shaddow that is vaine.
But rather raise thy thoughts a higher straine.
To GOD (I meane) who set this young-man free.
And in like straits can eke deliuer thee.

John Lilburne's account of his suffering and experience of God, with his portrait facing the title page.
(PRIVATE COLLECTION AND UK/BRIDGEMAN ART LIBRARY)

Twelve army officers and twelve Agitators met and crafted a moderate proposal that would return the king to his throne and remove bishops from the Church of England. Though this was a better deal than Charles had any right to expect, he responded with a typically arrogant and self-destructive outburst. "You cannot do this without me!" he pouted. "You fall to ruin if I do not sustain you." Colonel Rainborough made sure that the most angry and radical elements in the army learned of how dismissive the king had been.

Those radicals had a leader who was, in his way, as compelling as Winthrop and Cromwell. Like them, John Lilburne had found God when he was in misery. But this was no private agony. Lilburne discovered his mission in full view of his enemies. A fearless speaker and devout Puritan, Lilburne had been arrested by Archbishop Laud in 1637 and sentenced to be whipped through the streets of London, and then to stand, bleeding, in the Palace Yard at Westminster, before he was sent to prison. As he stood in the stocks and felt his wounds burn, Lilburne experienced a revelation.

Lilburne was "lifted up" by the Holy Spirit. It was not just that he felt the joyous presence of God; he suddenly understood the world in a new way. If God could choose a person as lowly as Lilburne, He could select anyone, so all were equal, leveled, before God. What law, rule, or noble blood could matter more than God? Though this was a religious experience, it had the potential of being an extremely radical political view. And after serving nobly beside Cromwell in the Civil War, Lilburne began making those views known.

When he was out of the Tower of London, Parliament found him as dangerous as had the king and archbishop. Led by Lilburne, the radicals began to hold meetings in London, training Agitators to spread their beliefs and hoping to win over the entire army. Conservatives took note of the name of another leader of this dangerous movement, for it seemed only too apt: John Wildman. Though Lilburne and Cromwell had served together and admired each other, the Levellers now began to call Cromwell and Ireton "Grandees," suggesting that they had become too much like their royal enemies. By October five regiments were strongholds of Leveller beliefs.

Viewed in one way, a small group of enlightened leaders was helping an army of free men to find its own true voice. John Milton put it this way:

"More just it is . . . that a less number compel a greater to retain . . . their liberty, than that a greater number . . . compel a less . . . to be their fellow-slaves." But looked at in another light, a cabal of extremists was plotting an army coup in which the traditional and elected government would be supplanted by revolutionaries and fanatics.

The astrologer William Lilly predicted that the end of October would bring "high and very great contentions . . . about our customs." He was right, for on October 28 Agitators, army officers, and the Grandees met at St. Mary the Virgin Church in Putney, just across the Thames from London, to debate England's future.

"THE POOREST HE"

On the day before the debate was to be held, agents from the five Leveller-dominated regiments spelled out their beliefs in "The Case of the Army, an Agreement of the People." This simple yet compelling document was the most democratic plan of government that had ever been proposed for England. Not until the twentieth century would England *or* America adopt such an inclusive system.

The "Agreement" argued that the entire basis of English government must be changed and agreed to by every single male householder over the age of twenty-one, with the significant exception of servants and beggars. Parliament was to be dissolved, the House of Lords eliminated, and the new body reelected every two years, which is exactly the plan later adopted for the American House of Representatives. Laws must apply to everyone equally, and "no tenure, estate, charter, degree, birth, or place" gave anyone special privileges. Just as John Hampden had argued in the ship money case, the king had no more rights than a common soldier. Religion was no longer to be a national matter, with rules imposed by king or Parliament. "Matters of Religion, and the ways of God's worship, are not at all entrusted by us to any human power."

These ideas may seem so uncontroversial—so "self-evident," as Jefferson put it in the Declaration of Independence—that it takes an act of historical imagination to see how new they were in 1647. At that time there was no country on Earth in which more than a few men had these rights. No one knew what it would be like to entirely give up the habit of assuming that nobles, wealthy men, and bishops knew what was best, and to trust any male who held property. When the United States drafted its Constitution, it deliberately created a Senate to balance the House, left the election of the president to the Electoral College, and expanded the nonvoting category of "servant" to include slaves. Even more than a century later, and after a war fought over the right of self-government, the ideas of the "Agreement" were too frightening to implement.

Cromwell knew exactly what would happen if the "Agreement" was adopted by the army. There would be a new and terrible civil war. The "Agreement," he argued, would fundamentally change the laws of the nation as they had existed "since it was a nation." No matter how valid the idea might be in the abstract, men must consider "whether . . . the spirits and temper of the people of this nation are prepared to receive and to go

Opposite: *The Levellers made use of pamphlets to express their grievances and to try to convert others to their cause. This effort to win people over through the party press was a new and powerful way of organizing.*   (THE FOTOMAS INDEX)

THE
Declaration and Standard

Of the *Levellers of England;*
Delivered in a Speech to his Excellency the Lord Gen. *Fairfax;*
on *Friday* laſt at White-Hall, by Mr. *Everard*, a late Member of the
Army, and his Propheſie in reference thereunto; ſhewing what will
befall the Nobility and Gentry of this Nation, by their ſubmitting to
community; With their invitation and promiſe unto the people, and
their proceedings in *Windſor* Park, *Oatlands* Park, and ſeverall other
places; alſo, the Examination and confeſſion of the ſaid Mr. *Everard*
before his Excellency, the manner of his deportment with his Hat on,
and his ſeverall ſpeeches and expreſſions, when he was commanded
to put it off. Together with a Liſt of the ſeverall Regiments of Horſe
and Foot that have caſt Lots to go for *Ireland.*

Imprinted at *London*, for *G. Laurenſon*, *Aprill* 23. 1649.

along with it." The paper might be called "An Agreement of the People," but it was no agreement if it was imposed on the nation by the army. Just as Thomas Dudley had warned that giving credence to every visionary would splinter Puritan New England, Cromwell feared that England itself would be shattered into separate states, each with its own agreement.

To Cromwell's radical critics, then and now, this was a betrayal, the worst betrayal of all. He had a chance to lead the people to freedom, and instead he turned into an executioner serving the conservative classes. Out of opportunism or fear he sold out; he was the Judas of the seventeenth century. That makes a great story, but it is probably wrong.

Cromwell was speaking for all moderates of all time—for John Winthrop, who exiled Williams and Hutchinson to save his colony; for James Madison, who traded the continuation of slavery for the unity of the thirteen colonies; for Booker T. Washington, who urged black Americans to focus on self-improvement and business rather than on battling southern whites for the right to vote. The question for such leaders is not just what is right in the abstract, but what people can accept.

In all likelihood Cromwell was right. England as a whole was not ready for democracy on such a scale. Men of even moderate wealth would have given anything to defeat the "Agreement," while great numbers of the poor were more focused on the advent of Jesus than on the right to vote. Had the army marched on London, as some Levellers demanded, the warfare that followed most probably would have resembled the bloody French Revolution, not the more moderate and pragmatic American revolt, to come less than a century and a half later.

And yet the most extreme Levellers spoke a truth that is particularly haunting to Americans. They sound like modern people trapped across the sea and out of time. When Lilburne continued the argument with Parliament two years later, he said, "I am sorry I have but one life to lose" in defense of his ideas. Whether or not Nathan Hale ever said the same thing is debated, but the phrase became a part of American history. At Putney, Ireton argued that only men of property should be allowed to vote, since poor people could be bought, and they would not have a real stake in society. A Leveller named Edward Sexby responded with a heartfelt expression of betrayal and abandonment. They had fought a difficult war, and now it seemed, "except a man has a fixed estate in this kingdom, he has no right in this kingdom—I wonder we were so much deceived! If we had not a right to the kingdom, we *were* mere mercenary soldiers."

The discussions went on long into the night. The following day's meeting took place not in the church but at the home of a Mr. Chamberlaine. And yet in a sense it was as much a prayer meeting as a political discussion. It began with five hours of prayer, as Cromwell and others earnestly sought divine guidance.

What an extraordinary moment: a roomful of captains, soldiers, a lieutenant general, the most vocal and argumentative men in England, all sitting together in silence as the hours went by, listening for the voice of God.

But when the holy silence ended, the afternoon turned into a four-sided argument among Cromwell, Ireton, Rainborough, and Wildman. Rainborough countered Cromwell's caution with simple eloquence: "I think that the poorest he that is in England hath a life to live as the greatest he, and therefore truly, Sir, I think it's clear, that every man that is to live under a government ought first by his own consent, to put himself under that government."

If there could be an instrument that measures changes in thought the way a seismograph tracks trembles in the earth, it would have spiked on that October afternoon. For while the "Agreement" was not adopted, and for the moment Cromwell and Ireton's moderation won out, a fundamental shift took place in the Putney Debates, as they were called. Cromwell kept listening for what God wanted—how people were ruled in this world did not matter to him, so long as it accorded with God's plan. Rainborough reversed those terms: God's plans were His business, but human beings deserved better government, and better lives. This was a fundamental change in the way people began to think about the world.

The implication of the "Agreement" was that the English Civil War had not been fought merely over bishops or presbyters; it was not just about Charles's divine right versus Parliament's rules. It was not even about the armies of Christ doing final battle against the Antichrist. Rather, if the war had brought with it a new age, it was because it opened up the possibility that each Englishman, every single one, could stake his own claim in the kingdom. It was not a war for God but for the rights of all men. As Wildman put it, "I conceive that's the undeniable maxim of government: that all government is in the free consent of the people." Reading Wildman and Rainborough, it is obvious that the pressure of war over king and God in England crystallized the ideas that gave birth to the United States of America.

AND SHE?

The four-sided argument led to the appointment of a committee to study the "Agreement." This did not please Wildman and the most extreme Levellers.

Instead, they circulated pamphlets in which Ireton and Cromwell were implicitly compared to the Devil, and soldiers were urged to mutiny, elect new officers, and create a new Parliament. The Devil rebelled against God, but the radicals believed they were upholding order, not overthrowing it. For they felt their victory was being stolen from them.

On November 15 the Levellers made their challenge explicit. When Fairfax and Cromwell arrived at the army camp, they were greeted with revolution in formation. Angry regiments had gathered, wearing copies of the "Agreement" in their hats, much like the field signs the army used in battle. "England's freedom! Soldier's right!" announced their emblems. This was a confrontation just one step short of mutiny. Cromwell might not know God's plans, but he knew how to discipline an army. He and his officers rode through the ranks, plucking the papers out. They identified four leaders and told them to choose which one would be executed. One man was shot, and a rebellion was quelled.

The Levellers' best chance to win over the army and transform the nation was over, but they continued to be an active force for some time, and in some new and startling ways. When in 1649 Parliament arrested several of their leaders, including Lilburne again, their wives organized a campaign to free them. This was not entirely surprising, as he had argued that women were "by nature all equal and alike in power, dignity, authority and majesty" to men. Sounding much like Winthrop disdaining Hutchinson, a legislator responded to the campaign with contempt: It was "not for women to petition, they might stay at home and wash their dishes." The argument that all adults are part of the nation and have a voice in its future was held by only a few radicals. Yet it was too powerful to be silenced that easily.

Katherine Chidley was a former preacher who had become a Leveller. She argued that "considering that we have an equal share and interest with men in the Commonwealth and it cannot be laid waste (as it now is) and not we be the greatest and most helpless sufferers therein; and considering that poverty, misery, and famine, like a mighty torrent is breaking upon us . . . and we are not able to see our children hang upon us, and cry out for bread, and not have wherewithal to feed them, we had rather die than see that day." Just as war over British Heaven had forced the army to consider the rights of the "poorest he," the conflict gave some women the courage to speak up for themselves.

Chapter Twelve

The Inner Light

"Behold the Head of a Traitor"

Cromwell's choice to trust in God's plans rather than give in to the political demands of men and women shaped England's future. For he faced a series of crises and, each time, resolved them by seeking divine guidance. But just as he thought he was finally able to lead England to heed God, the vexing results led him and others to question this entire approach to governing a nation. Just as the Levellers were too far ahead of their time, Cromwell's moments of triumph really only proved that his way of thinking was an artifact of the past.

Even as Cromwell was debating with the Levellers in 1647, Charles escaped from the army. The king decided it was time to stop playing off potential partners and to choose an ally. This was his last, and fatal, mistake. He selected Scotland, promising that he would ensure that Presbyterianism would rule in England for a three-year test period, and that the Independents would be suppressed. The Civil War began again, with scattered supporters of the king rising up in England while the Scots were to invade from the north, this time in support of the king. The New Model Army crushed the local revolts, which left Fairfax and Cromwell to solve the puzzle of the three kingdoms that had eluded Charles. They controlled England, but Scotland was allied with the king, and Ireland seemed entirely lost.

In August 1648 Cromwell, leading just 8,600 men against 14,000 Scots soldiers, decided this second phase of the Civil War. He had marched his men to northern England, and near the city of Preston he attacked with disciplined fury. He chose to place his troops north of the enemy, so that they could not retreat into Scotland. Then he used his smaller forces as an advantage. The Scots were spread out in a wide line. Cromwell concentrated his men, which meant they would overwhelm the enemy wherever they faced off. Though his men suffered many injuries, only about 100 were killed, while, over three days of fighting and pursuit, 10,000 of the enemy were taken prisoner. Having accomplished such a complete and devastating victory, Cromwell saw "the great hand of God in this business."

God was directing Cromwell and the army to defeat His enemies—but which enemies? The king had cast his lot with Scotland; did that make him an enemy? Many in the army were sure they knew. The kind of pamphlets that spread Leveller thought now argued that Charles was exactly the sort of tyrant God condemned in the Bible. And God would not forgive those who failed to execute his judgments. One member of Parliament explained that if they did not execute the king, it would "draw down the just vengeance of God upon us all." But Cromwell was not convinced. And as clear as this mandate was to one faction, it was hateful to another. The Cavalier poet Richard Lovelace wrote from prison,

I would love a Parliament
As a main prop from Heaven sent;
But ah! Who's he that would be wedded
To the fairest body that's beheaded.

If Charles was tried and convicted, he would lose his head. But Lovelace might have had something more than that in mind.

Facing a Parliament that was still exploring negotiations with the once-again imprisoned sovereign, the army acted. On December 6, 1648, the aptly named Colonel Thomas Pride stood by the door of Westminster Hall, where Parliament met, and prevented members whom the army opposed from entering the building. Parliament itself, you might say, was beheaded, for nearly half its members were excluded and more than forty sent to prison. The remaining small subset, or Rump, of Parliament then created a commission to try Charles.

By the beginning of 1649 Cromwell finally thought he understood what God required of him, and of England: Charles I, the man responsible for all the deaths and miseries of the two Civil Wars, must be executed. In the Bible's Book of Numbers, chapter 25, God saved Israel because Phinehas meted out justice himself, killing a couple whose lovemaking was sinful. Cromwell had come to believe that he was a modern Phinehas, required to kill a king to save a kingdom from God's wrath.

One hundred fifty commissioners were appointed to judge the king, but so many resisted that the number was reduced by fifteen, and at the first ses-

The Tryal of the King.

The Army having purg'd the House of Commons and left none but their own Creatures to sit there, appointed a Committee for ye Kings Tryal wth began 20 Jan: 1648, on which day 67 Commissioners were present and when Genl Fairfax's Name was called over, his Lady cryed out He has more Wit than to be here, and when he was Indited in the Name of all the good People of England she also Cryed out, no nor one hundred part of them, his Gold Head dropt from his Cane, this day without any visible cause, on the 2d 70 Commissioners were present, as were 71 on the 3d day, and 66 on the 4th when Bradshaw pronounced the Sentence.

This later depiction of the trial of the king captures the claustrophobic intensity of the event. Charles's nobility and courage in facing his judges and his executioner won more people to his side than at any other point in his reign. (THE FOTOMAS INDEX)

sion only fifty-two appeared. Only a third of the justices handpicked by Cromwell's carefully purged Parliament were willing to judge the man held responsible for two terrible wars.

The king's trial began on January 20, 1649, but, as in the treason trials of

Essex, Ralegh, and Strafford, this was not really an investigation. Once Charles was brought to court, there was no doubt that he would be convicted. By January 26 the warrant for his execution was being circulated among the judges. Years later many claimed that they were pressured, forced by Cromwell himself, into signing the deadly paper. That may be true, since it was typical of him to dismiss all opposition once he had set on a course. But the reason for his conviction was not personal gain. He believed that he must kill Charles to save England, as he had executed a few Levellers to keep control of the army.

On January 30, the date set for his execution, Charles carried himself with grace and dignity. It was a very cold day, and he wore two shirts so that he would not shiver and seem to be afraid. He spoke softly to his chaplain, defending his reign and committing himself to God. The executioner did his duty, then lifted the sliced-off head for all to see. "Behold the head of a traitor."

DIGGERS, RANTERS, BAPTISTS, QUAKERS, AND THE ARMY OF SAINTS

Killing the king inspired two opposite reactions. For some it was profoundly disturbing, a violation of all English law and tradition. For others it was a crucial step on the timetable of the millennium. The very act of killing the king, of ending the monarchy and establishing a new commonwealth, suggested that a new age had begun. But what should the new rules be, in God's new age?

A failed cloth seller named Gerrard Winstanley began to have visions.

He believed the Levellers did not go far enough. It was not merely that all men should vote: Property should be taken away from the wealthy and shared among all. "True religion and undefiled is to let everyone quietly have earth to manure, that they may live in freedom by their labors. . . . Money," he insisted, "must not any longer . . . be the great god that hedges some in and hedges others out." Those who followed him in establishing what we might now call Christian-socialist communes were called Diggers. (In the 1960s a new group in San Francisco took the same name. They too attempted to give up money, handed out free food, and sought personal liberation. It would not be surprising if a set of antiglobalization, proenvironmental activists were to pay homage to these ancestors and revive the name again in the twenty-first century.)

A step beyond the Diggers were the Ranters. Like the Family of Love, they believed that those who were truly saved were completely above the law. They could swear horrible oaths—which gave them their name—have sex with whomever they wanted, and never fear that they were violating God's law. Since they were chosen, anything they did was right.

John Lilburne was imprisoned for the last time in 1653. While in jail he joined yet another new religious group, the Children of Light, or, as they became known, the Religious Society of Friends. Founded by a wandering preacher named George Fox, the group trusted in an inner sense perhaps similar to the one that had animated Anne Hutchinson. They tried to open themselves to this inner light, and as it washed over them, some would shake or spontaneously begin to sing. This involuntary motion gave the group its most familiar name, Quakers. They did not have a political program like the Levellers or Diggers, but they believed all could be saved by the Holy Spirit. For a time they allowed women to preach, and they rejected the kind of social distinctions in which the humble were expected to defer to their "betters." The movement grew quickly and inspired converts to demonstrate their faith: some fasted, a few tried to perform miracles, and others arrived in church naked.

The Quakers, like another new sect that arose at this time, the Baptists, survived, while the Ranters and Diggers did not. Quakers made converts in the middling ranks of people, the very sorts who could afford the passage to the New World, and they even found support in those wealthy enough to establish new colonies. In an altered form the ideas of the Levellers, the democratic vision of government outlined in the "Agreement of the People," came to America with the Quakers.

There was nothing more frightening to the New England Puritans than the Quakers. They were an entire sect of Anne Hutchinsons, trusting their own inner voices, shaking, as perhaps the Devil himself made them do, and trying to spread their beliefs in the Land of Promise. The first Quakers arrived in New England in 1656 and were immediately suspected of being witches. One minister termed the Quakers' inner light "a stinking vapor from Hell." Two years later two Quakers who returned to Boston after having been whipped and banished each had an ear cut off. The Massachusetts colony passed a law prescribing a death sentence for any who returned from banishment, precisely to deter just such determined and devoted Quaker missionaries.

Severe punishments were no more effective at stamping out the Puritans' enemies than when Charles used them to try to control Puritanism itself. By 1674 there was a Quaker meetinghouse in Boston. Quaker communities flourished in Rhode Island, where Anne Hutchinson's sister welcomed them; in Maryland; and most famously in Pennsylvania. Just as the size of

THE QVAKERS DREAM: 14

OR,
The Devil's Pilgrimage in England:
BEING

An infallible Relation of their several Meetings,

Shreekings, Shakings, Quakings, Roarings, Yellings, Howlings, Tremblings in the Bodies, and Riuings in the Bellies: With a Narrative of their several Arguments, Tenets, Principles, and strange Doctrine: The strange and wonderful Satanical Apparitions, and the appearing of the Devil unto them in the likeness of a black Boar, a Dog with flaming eyes, and a black man without a head, causing the Dogs to bark, the Swine to cry, and the Cattel to run, to the great admiration of all that shall read the same.

London, Printed for G. Horton, and are to be sold at the Royal Exchange in Cornhil, 1655. Aprill. 26.

America had allowed Roger Williams to leave Boston and establish a new colony, it ensured that any group of believers, no matter how despised by others, could take root and flourish.

As these alternate forms of faith took hold, Cromwell had a more immediate religious and political problem to solve: Ireland. Like Elizabeth, James, and Charles before him, he needed to bring that difficult island under control. Unlike his predecessors, he succeeded.

EFFUSIONS OF BLOOD

Cromwell's war in Ireland left scars that are felt to this day. He believed the stories of Irish massacres that had accompanied the rebellion in 1641. He was sure the Irish had "put the English to the most unheard-of and most barbarous massacre (without respect of sex and age) that ever the sun beheld." He also trusted in the military strategy of terror that the Puritans had used in the Pequot War: Show how merciless you can be once, and you will have fewer battles to fight later. When he arrived at the walled city of Drogheda, he gave it an ultimatum: His army would "reduce it to obedience," which would bring an "effusion of blood," unless it surrendered immediately. The defenders, who historians now believe were mainly the Protestant Royalist army of the Duke of Ormonde, not Irish Catholics, chose to resist. This was a terrible mistake.

At Drogheda, Cromwell showed what merciless could be. He "forbade" his soldiers "to spare any that were in arms in the town, and, I think, that

Opposite: *Enemies of the Quakers accused them of being as extreme in their behavior as the Family of Love.* (PRIVATE COLLECTION AND UK/BRIDGEMAN ART LIBRARY)

night they put to the sword about two thousand men." Historians believe the total killed was perhaps 1,000 more than that. When his army came to Wexford, Cromwell did face Irish Catholics, but he and the local leader were negotiating a truce when guns were fired. This time even Cromwell was not in control of his men, and the English killed some 2,000 people in a riot of death and devastation that was no longer simply a military contest. Some of the prisoners taken in the city were sent on to Barbados as slaves. From the standpoint of Irish Catholic myth and memory, Cromwell was the very opposite of the agent of God—rather, he was the bearer of murder, destruction, and enslavement.

Cromwell returned to England in 1650 as a hero. All the more so the following year, when he routed the combined forces of the Scots and Prince Charles, son of the executed king. As a general he was invincible. With his popularity and the sense of mission he gave his troops, it seemed that if ever Saints could rule, the time was now. There was only one problem: The Rump Parliament was still sitting, and even though the members had been carefully screened, they were grumbling, difficult politicians.

Cromwell could do what Charles could only have imagined. In 1653 he personally removed the sitting members of Parliament and insisted that new ones be chosen from a list prepared by approved Independent ministers. The new Parliament of Saints met for the first time on July 4. "Truly," he told the devout members, "you are called by God to rule with him and for him." In a sense he was creating by force what Winthrop had established by crossing the ocean—a community run by and for the godly. Parliament immediately became preoccupied with deals, disputes, factions. Sounding again like Winthrop, Cromwell pleaded that "if every one (instead of contending) would justify his form of judgment by love and meekness, wisdom" would

The destruction of Drogheda. (THE FOTOMAS INDEX)

reign. Within five months the Parliament of Saints resigned, and Cromwell was appointed Lord Protector. Though he refused to accept the title of King, he had in essence become another Charles: a ruler with a strong sense of what was good for his nation but who was unable to get his legislators to stop behaving like politicians and to cooperate with him. After the failure of even the Saints to bring about the end of days and the return of Jesus, Cromwell lost some of his confidence that those awesome events were about to happen.

When he was sure he knew what God wanted, Cromwell was an inspired general who won battle after battle, no matter how strong an opponent he faced. He was able to defeat enemies in England, Scotland, and Ireland, execute a king, purge and then personally reconstruct Parliament. But none of these successes brought about the return of Jesus, and without that divine help, he could not create an enduring government.

Critics of Cromwell and the Commonwealth believed it stood for everything bad in an oppressive government supported by a powerful army. Ever since his time, politicians in England, and later in the United States, have been concerned with limiting the power of the army, and with ensuring that it serves rather than directs government policy. (THE FOTOMAS INDEX)

LEGACIES

Oliver Cromwell died in 1658, and his son Richard followed him as Lord Protector. But within two years Charles's son had returned to England as its new ruler, Charles II. Neither the army nor Parliament would fight for Richard or against Charles. What, then, had been accomplished by two Civil Wars, invasions back and forth across the Scottish border, and the destruction of Ireland's cities? One Charles had ruled at the beginning, another at the end.

The godly, even when led by an inspired general and a devout army, could not turn a nation of humans into a kingdom of God. No amount of spiritual perfection or military force could bring that about. Instead, Cromwell spoke for liberty of conscience and the worthiness of all men; Levellers extended this inclusive approach to politics, Diggers to economics, and Quakers to the language of the soul. The greatest legacy of the rule of the godly in England is that it failed. During the rest of the century, as political parties began to form in England, writers repeatedly warned against letting power accumulate in a permanently mobilized army, in the church, in big cities, or anywhere else where it might run out of control. Toleration, difference of opinion, the idea that all should have a say in government rather than all live as a single nation united before God—these were the products of Cromwell's career. In 1689 Charles II's Catholic son, James II, was forced from his throne by the Protestant William of Orange and his wife, Mary. As a condition of their reign they agreed to rule in combination with Parliament and to allow legislators freedom of speech.

In New England, in 1649, John Winthrop died, the same year as Charles I. The passing of the first generation of leaders brought with it a

When Charles II came to power, Cromwell was portrayed as the worst of villains, a man who had attempted to destroy English liberty.   (THE FOTOMAS INDEX)

larger problem. Not enough of the faithful were coming to church with the same certainty as their parents that they had been saved. A new generation was not as sure it was undergoing the conversion experiences that had been decisive for Cromwell and Winthrop. Throughout the rest of the century ministers in New England debated relaxing their standards for church membership. And when William and Mary took power, the new rulers insisted that the brand of religious toleration they practiced at home be observed across the Atlantic.

If New England was a Land of Promise, it was not because of its strength of faith or uniformity of practice. Just as the rule of Saints failed in England, it proved impossible in New England. On both continents extremists posed challenges to godly rulers, which forced the leaders to choose order over purity. On both continents that left it to legislators to work out rules of government, and to believers to seek their own salvation.

EPILOGUE

BRITISH HELL, AMERICAN PROMISE

THE REBEL

King Charles and John Winthrop, the Presbyterian Scots and the Independent Cromwell, all had one thing in common. They believed they were seeking to return Christianity to its true and original form. No matter if they were in government or fighting against it, they saw themselves as the loyal guardians of a timeless truth. They were certainly not rebels, for to be a rebel meant to seek to overturn the existing order, and that was horrible. After all, the worst crime that had ever taken place came when Satan rebelled against God—and brought evil into the world.

All the enemies in the English Civil War agreed that good would come when true order was restored, either with the arrival of King Jesus or the return of King Charles. Everyone would see the truth, and error would be punished, either by a person's conscience or, as

Winthrop warned Hutchinson, by the community, which would keep her conscience for her. But even though they themselves did not know it, the religious toleration that Williams, Cromwell, and the Levellers favored contained the hint of another view. Different people might have different ideas of truth. Perhaps no single truth would be evident to all. And if that was so, being a rebel would not necessarily be bad. It might be that the existing order was false, and only a complete change could remedy that. But if that was so in human affairs, what about in the Bible itself? Could it be that Satan was a hero?

John Milton lived through the rise of the godly under the leadership of an inspired man, and then saw even the Saints fall. In being a part of those events, and telling the story of Satan's fall, Milton made a fundamental discovery about human nature. He mapped out the states of pride, defiance, anger, in which we would rather destroy than build; in which we are magnificent in our darkness, not in our love of light.

Milton's greatest work is *Paradise Lost*. It is about Lucifer, the fallen angel, and begins just after his descent from Heaven when he is farthest from God. It is a portrait of a creature whose will is so strong that he will never submit to God. If God seeks to bring good even out of evil, "our labor must be to pervert that end." Milton made his Satan so strong, so intense, so real, that even though he is the very incarnation of evil, he is also more vivid and compelling than God. Anyone who has ever been defiant in defeat and reveled in being in a hateful state of mind will recognize Milton's insightfulness:

> *Farewell, happy fields*
> *Where joy for ever dwells: Hail horrors, hail*
> *Infernal world . . .*

Though God has defeated him, Satan has one last and most precious freedom. He can choose *not* to be good, and to embrace an eternity of misery. In the depths of his exile from all goodness and beauty, Satan swears, "Better to reign in Hell, than serve in Heaven."

Through the figure of Satan, Milton captured the psychology of the rebel, the person who would overturn all creation if his pride, his ambition, his will demanded it. His Satan is riveting because he is so real, so recognizable. He is a part of us, and of our world. Every antihero since—in fiction, movies, music—follows in his pattern. A decade of hope for the arrival of Jesus and wars over souls crystallized in one poet an image of the side of human beings that ever resists salvation.

Religious communities in a new land, just like Parliaments of Saints in the homeland, could make their rules as pure as they liked, and enforce them with exile, whipping, war, but they would all fail. They sought to enforce perfection on Earth, and did not recognize the appeal of destruction, of imperfection, of reigning in Hell rather than serving in Heaven. The great creations of an age of religious passion and hope were not perfect societies; rather, they were Milton's Satan and the democratic ideas expressed in the "Agreement of the People." And yet the religious yearnings have endured—and brought their own triumphs.

THE GLORY

The kind of spiritual awakening that John Cotton had inspired when he arrived in Boston flared up again in the British colonies whenever a particularly inspired or passionate preacher arrived. The most famous of these Great Awakenings began in the 1730s in Connecticut and New Jersey, and flowered in the 1740s, when the compelling preacher George Whitefield visited. As he toured through the colonies, his strong, powerful voice, the dramatic presentation, and his personal charisma aroused parishioners to experience a new birth, which led some to roll in the aisles, declare their sins, and accept their salvation.

When Whitefield reached into parts of Virginia, though, planters were reluctant to have him preach to the slaves. They blamed his religious revival for inspiring the slave revolt that took place in New York in 1741. But by 1776 mixed congregations of blacks and whites in Virginia were joining in new revivals. As one missionary reported, "hundreds fell to the ground, and the house seemed to shake with the presence of God. The chapel was full of white and black." Though slave masters made it illegal to teach reading and writing to the people they treated as property, these services spread the messages and stories of the Bible. By the end of the eighteenth century so many enslaved people had been exposed to the Bible that they began to see their history in it.

The enslaved people who listened to sermons, and created songs—spirituals—based on the characters in the Bible, and told and retold Bible stories to each other, were very much like the English people in the 1640s poring over their King James Bibles. They were getting the truth, the Good News, for the first time, and they heard their enslavement explained and their redemption promised.

Now the story of the Land of Promise, which had brought John Winthrop and Roger Williams and Anne Hutchinson to North America, took on a new meaning. Africans in America were literally slaves, as the Jews had been in Egypt, as the Puritans had seen themselves when they were in the England of King Charles I. For the African Americans the Promised

Land was sometimes linked to Africa, or to free states, or to the north where a person could be free. But it was not merely a physical place; it was also a state of mind—it was the condition of being free. That meaning of the Promised Land remains a powerful part of American life.

On April 3, 1968, the night before he was killed, the Reverend Martin Luther King Jr. seemed to sense that his life was nearing its end. He spoke of his mission and that he might not live to see it fulfilled. "I've been to the mountaintop. . . . And I've looked over, and I've seen the Promised Land. I may not get there with you, but I want you to know tonight that we as a people will get to the Promised Land." The Promised Land he spoke of was the land of the American dream, the land of freedom for all.

The wars of the seventeenth century proved to most that God was not going to lead any one group in England or in America to a physical place of ultimate salvation. It would be up to fallible human beings to create a better, more promising land on their own. Edmund Waller, a poet who first served in Parliament and later sided with King Charles I, understood that the failure of grand dreams brought the beginning of new possibilities. He had seen firsthand the price paid for religious passion, and he was a lifelong advocate of toleration. He wrote:

> Stronger by weakness, wiser men become,
> As they draw near their eternal home.
> Leaving the old, both worlds at once they view,
> That stand upon the threshold of the new.

Waller was writing about the new world of Heaven that we reach after death. But his verses also apply to the New World. It took well over another century after the time of John Winthrop and Oliver Cromwell for America to be born as a separate nation. But throughout the rest of our history descendents of Indians and Europeans, enslaved people and slave masters, religious visionaries and passionate atheists—all have had to measure their old ideas against the new conditions of a new world, and only in that never-ending process of growth and change fulfill the promise of this land.

ENDNOTES AND BIBLIOGRAPHY

WHY THIS BOOK

p. xiii   For Protestants encouraging people to be martyrs, see Anna R. Beer, *Sir Walter Ralegh and His Readers in the Seventeenth Century: Speaking to the People* (New York: St. Martin's, 1997), p. 125. This is an academic study that is aimed at professionals. I give examples of calls for war against Charles, and of religious radicals destroying images, in this book.

PROLOGUE: WHO RULES ENGLAND?

p. 1   I found the complete text of the royal masque *Salmacida Spolia* on the Internet at www.shakespeare.bham.ac.uk/masque/SalmacidaSpolia.htm (I am omitting http://, which precedes each URL). In trying to learn more about the costumes, I was led to the fascinating site www.costumes.org/pages/17thlinks.htm, which is a wonderful jumping-off place for research; it also includes costume.dm.net/wardrobe/masque.html, in which a modern woman has reconstructed a costume for a sixteenth-century masque and described in detail her materials and methods.

p. 3   An excellent Internet source that gives current views on the history of the Book of Revelation, as well as informative discussions on many ways it has been interpreted, is www.pbs.org/wgbh/pages/frontline/shows/apocalypse/explanation/brevelation.html, which is drawn from a PBS show on the topic and includes short questions and answers from many experts. Another useful site is www.lib.virginia.edu/speccol/exhibits/brimstone/england.html. This not only gives a short, easy-to-follow account of the importance of the Book of Revelation in the conflicts of the seventeenth century in England and New England but also includes images of title pages of some of the more significant historical texts of the time.

p. 5   For the story of Mr. Crab, including the link to the phrase about hatters, see Christopher Hill, *Puritanism and Revolution: Studies in Interpretation of the English Revolution of the Seventeenth Century* (New York: St. Martin's, 1997), pp. 282–89. Though easy to read and filled with fascinating stories that would be hard to find anywhere else, the collection will be of use primarily to readers who already know the main themes and personalities of the English Civil War. I discuss Hill in more detail below, in the note to p. 31. Another possible source for the phrase is that hat makers were exposed to mercury vapor, which poisoned them and made them seem daft.

THE GODLY

CHAPTER ONE: THE BRITISH HEAVEN

p. 10   On *Histrio-Mastix,* see Stephen Orgel and Roy Strong, eds., *Inigo Jones, The Theatre of the Stuart Court* [hereafter IJ], 2 vols. (London: Sotheby Park Bernet, and Berkeley, Calif.: University of California Press, 1973), p. 51. This is a book for specialists. But any young reader interested in the history of theater, or in Charles I and his lavish court, will have the marvelous treat of seeing original drawings and sketches of Jones's innovative sets and costumes.

p. 11   For Prynne's views on the right to overthrow, see Simon Schama, *A History of Britain* [hereafter HB], vol. II (New York: Hyperion, Talk Miramax Books, 2001), p. 99. The second volume of a three-volume grand-scale history of England written by a well-known historian to accompany a TV series, this is accessible, well illustrated, and a reasonable place for a young reader who wants to know more to begin a search; for Prynne's anti-Semitism, see Derek Hirst, "The Lord Protector," in John

Morrill, ed., *Oliver Cromwell and the English Revolution* (London and New York: Longmans, 1990), p. 137; on the king and law, see Johann Sommerville, "Oliver Cromwell and English Political Thought," in the same volume, p. 240. This collection of academic articles on Cromwell by leading historians was very useful to me, as it included thoughtful and current evaluations of aspects of his life. Though I doubt it will be of much use or interest to young readers, it is an important reminder of how dynamic history is—a constant process of evaluation and reevaluation.

p. 13   I found much useful material on Hampden on the Internet, for example at www.skyhook.co.uk/civwar/biog/hampden.htm. This is an excellent site devoted to the English Civil War and has many useful resources on it. The caution readers need to keep in mind is that, as I explain in this book, the English Civil War is still a highly controversial subject in England, with partisans who feel strongly about who was right and who was wrong. Thus the Hampden who appears on the site of the John Hampden Society is a great hero. I didn't find a matching site that calls him a villain, but the tone of the society is especially reverential. Read English sites devoted to their Civil War with the same alert skepticism you might have for an American site about our Civil War. If you landed on a site that had an animated Confederate flag proudly waving, for example, you'd be able to guess what it would have to say. A similar tip-off on English sites will be the language they use to describe their war—as a heroic conflict over rights and liberties, or as a clash between calculating legislators and a martyred, earnest king.

p. 14   For the king and the law, see Sir Charles Firth, *Oliver Cromwell and the Rule of the Puritans in England* [hereafter OCRP] (London: Oxford University Press, 1900; World's Classics Edition, 1961), pp. 20–21. This highly readable account is based on the work of Samuel Rawson Gardiner, a nineteenth-century historian whose writings are the foundation of all modern work on the English Civil War. Long viewed as hopelessly old-fashioned, Gardiner has come back into favor, as modern scholars appreciate his breadth of knowledge and the solidity of his basic understanding. In the manner of nineteenth-century histories, this is quite easy to read, and it has none of the forbidding academic vocabulary of modern texts. It is a wonderful place to start. Readers should, though, be aware that specialized studies of nearly everything discussed in the book have since been published, and each of them shades and complicates this view. Begin here, but don't end here.

p. 15   The subhead "No Bishop, No King" is a famous remark of James I. See Mark Kishlansky, *A Monarchy Transformed: Britain 1603–1714* [hereafter AMT] (London and New York: Penguin, 1997), p. 73. Kishlansky is a prominent member of a group of relatively younger scholars who have taken a new look at the history of this era. This book is a summary written for a general audience. It reads well for the alert high school reader. See note for p. 29, though, for a comparison of some numbers he uses with those cited by another scholar.

pp. 15-17 The description of the masque follows that in *The Poems of Thomas Carew with his Masque Coelum Britannicum*, Rhodes Dunlap, ed. [hereafter PTC], (Oxford, England: Clarendon, 1949), pp. 151–85. For the importance of this masque, see IJ, p. 66.

p. 20   On Scotland and the origin of "clan," see Fitzroy Maclean, *Scotland: A Concise History* [hereafter SAC] (London: Thames & Hudson, 1970; 2nd rev. ed., 2000), p. 66.

p. 20   This religious history is recounted in SAC, pp. 91–93; for Knox on women, see SAC, p. 92.

p. 21   For Ralegh's history in Ireland, see my *Sir Walter Ralegh and the Quest for El Dorado* [hereafter SWR] (New York: Clarion, 2000), p. 81.

p. 21   For the history of the Ulster Scots, including the later migration to America, see Robert McCrum, William Cran, and Robert MacNeil, *The Story of English* (New York: Penguin, 1987; rev. ed., 1993), pp. 137–47. Written to accompany a TV series, this is a very readable and engaging book with many gems in it for high school readers. As it shows, within the history of language is every other form of history.

CHAPTER TWO: JOHN WINTHROP

p. 23   For Puritan preaching, see Francis J. Bremer, *The Puritan Experiment: New England Society from Bradford to Edwards* [hereafter PE] (New York: St. Martin's, 1976; rev. ed., Hanover, NH: University Press of New England, 1995), pp. 24–26.

This is a survey on the Puritans that is probably most useful for college courses. But high school students will also find it to be a handy and well-informed reference.

p. 24   On the history of the Bible in this period, see Christopher Hill, *The English Bible and the Seventeenth-Century Revolution* [hereafter EB] (London and New York: Penguin, 1993); for the one million Bibles, see p. 18. Hill was one of the great historians of the English Civil War period. His passion was for the radicals, those critics who wanted to expand the reformation of society to include changes in class structure. He brought their views back into the center of historical discussion, and in the 1970s he was the acknowledged master of this field. Since then a wave of historians has challenged his theoretical approach and many details within it. In particular, his emphasis on class as an explanation of events in this period is no longer widely accepted; instead, religion is given more importance. In addition, detailed studies of particular people and groups have undermined some of his more sweeping arguments. Still, he was unparalleled in his command of the written sources of the period and is always well worth reading. While the book assumes a basic knowledge of English history that most American high school readers do not have, it has so many fascinating stories and examples in it that I urge the motivated reader to give it a try anyway.

p. 25   For this description of the Winthrop estate, see Edmund Sears Morgan, *The Puritan Dilemma: The Story of John Winthrop* [hereafter PD] (Boston: Little, Brown, 1958), p. 3. Morgan is one of the two foremost contemporary scholars of the colonial period (the other is Bernard Bailyn), and his work is a pleasure to read. This book is an excellent short biography of Winthrop. It was designed for general readers or undergraduates but should present few problems for high school readers.

pp. 25–26 For Winthrop's resolutions, see PD, pp. 9–10, and Charles Lloyd Cohen, *God's Caress: The Psychology of Puritan Religious Experience* [hereafter GC] (New York: Oxford, 1986), pp. 246–47. Cohen's book is aimed at a college or graduate school audience, and I recommend it only for students who have some background on the Puritans or for teachers preparing a class. That said, it is a thoughtful, articulate, deeply researched book, which has had a great influence on my thinking and is one of the most insightful books on the Puritans in the last twenty years. His "case study" of

Winthrop is the foundation of my understanding of the man and his faith. Cohen taught at New York University for one semester when I was in graduate school, and his class was an inspiration to me.

p. 26 Marvell was a Puritan whose poetry often deals with the struggle between the soul and the vividly depicted attractions of this world. These lines are from a poem called "A Dialogue Between the Resolved Soul and Created Pleasure," which is entirely about this conflict. Though the title and thrust of the poem lean toward the soul's argument, his most famous poem, "To His Coy Mistress," makes the opposite case. For Marvell's poem, see John T. Shawcross and Ronald David Emma, eds., *Seventeenth-Century English Poetry* [hereafter SEP] (Philadelphia: Lippincott, 1969), pp. 414–16. One of the treats of studying this period is the poetry, and I urge readers to browse through collections such as this to see what strikes their fancy.

p. 27 For the surprising fact that the average age at first marriage for men in this period was twenty-eight, see J. A. Sharpe, *Early Modern England: A Social History, 1550–1760* [hereafter EME] (London: Arnold, 1987; 2nd ed., 1997), p. 39. This is a survey of scholarship written for undergraduate readers. It is very useful as an introduction to key issues that historians are considering and debating, but it does presume a basic knowledge of the period. I found it fascinating, and I highly recommend it for teachers or other adults needing to refresh their knowledge and to catch up on more recent views.

p. 27 For Winthrop's conversion experience, see GC, pp. 247–50.

pp. 28–29 On the debate over possible changes in marriage, see EME, pp. 61–69. For Carew's poem, see PTC, pp. 12–13.

p. 29 On the rural population of England, see AMT, p. 6. In discussing the same trends, Kishlansky's book is a step more accessible than Sharpe's more clearly college-age text, EME. But when he and Sharpe discuss the same statistically based topics, Sharpe's numbers are always more nuanced and precise.

pp. 29–30 On the practice of "skimmington" or "riding the stang," see EME, pp. 94–95. That fascinating example comes up even as Sharpe tries to disprove an older view that the villagers were malicious, grim people given to mob violence. This idea, developed by historian Lawrence Stone, was itself an effort to correct the image of England from Henry VIII on as a "merry" place, where people lived happy, peaceful lives. Sharpe finds both models too extreme and cites many local studies that express more subtle views of strife and cooperation.

p. 31   On the population growth in London, see EME, p. 84. On the changes in village society, see EME, pp. 90–101. Sharpe is skeptical about older and more simplistic models of social change in this period.

pp. 32–34 For Protestant interpretations of biblical prophecies, see PE, p. 42.

CHAPTER THREE: A LAND OF PROMISE

p. 35   For the chapter title, see John Cotton, "God's Promise to His Plantations," in Alan Heimert and Andrew Delbanco, eds., *The Puritans in America: A Narrative Anthology* [hereafter PiA] (Cambridge, Mass.: Harvard University Press, 1985), p. 77. This is an excellent anthology of primary sources with thoughtful commentary from two leading scholars. The tone of the comments presumes a college-level background in this material, but even younger readers will find it a very useful compendium of primary sources.

p. 36   For Winthrop on the Indians, see his "Reasons to Be Considered for . . . the Intended Plantation in New England," in PiA, p. 73.

p. 37   For Cotton, "God's Promise," see PiA, p. 77.

p. 38   On plague, see PiA, p. 77. For the effects of the epidemic, see Albert A. Cave, *The Pequot War* [hereafter PW] (Amherst, Mass.: University of Massachusetts, 1996), p. 43. This recent and thorough study of the Pequot War has challenged generations of myth and misunderstanding. Brought to my attention by Dr. Bremer, it significantly changed my view of the war and it should be the starting place for anyone interested in learning more about the events Cave describes. For Hariot on disease, see SWR, p. 75.

pp. 39–40 For Winthrop on the Lord's wrath and for the following quotations from "A Model of Christian Charity," see PiA, pp. 82–92.

p. 41   For the subhead "A Great Marvel," as well as the quotes on pp. 45–46 and 47, see Winthrop in PD, p. 68. This section on Winthrop's first year in New England is drawn from PD, chapter 5, "Survival," pp. 54–68. Readers curious to know more would do well to read Morgan's account for themselves.

p. 43   For "idle" and "return," see PD, p. 58. The English settlers did not believe water that was standing still, not moving, was safe to drink.

p. 45   For "infectious persons," see TC, p. 163.

p. 48   On life expectancy in New England and Virginia, see AMT, pp. 10–11. For "fat hogs," see PD, p. 68.

pp. 48–49 For a brief useful summary of the evolution of government in Massachusetts, see PE, pp. 58–62 and PD, pp. 40–41.

Chapter Four: Conscience

p. 50   For Anne Bradstreet, see Andrew Delbanco, *The Puritan Ordeal* [hereafter PO] (Cambridge, Mass.: Harvard University Press, 1989), p. 137. This is, again, a college-level discussion of the issue. It is also challenging, intelligent, and well worth reading for anyone wanting to study this period in depth. For Roger Clap, the quoted settler, on the early days, see David D. Hall, ed., intro., *The Antinomian Controversy, 1636–1638: A Documentary History* [hereafter AC] (Durham, N.C.: Duke University Press, 1990), p. 13. Hall's commentaries are readable and learned but will prove most useful to teachers or advanced students. The documents themselves are excellent resources for anyone wanting to follow this important story from the original sources.

p. 51   The most recent and thorough study of the religious conflicts in this period is Michael P. Winship, *Making Heretics: Militant Protestantism and Free Grace in Massachusetts, 1636–1641* [hereafter MH] (Princeton, N.J.: Princeton University Press, 2002), another work brought to my attention by Dr. Bremer. The book is filled with learned and fresh insights and is sure to be read by every graduate student and professor interested in this period. But it is written for those entirely familiar with the subtle theological debates of the day. For hot Protestants, see MH, p. 3; on the Family of Love, see MH, p. 25; for Underhill and tobacco, see PW, p. 140.

p. 51   As readers of my *Witch-Hunt: Mysteries of the Salem Witch Trials* (New York: Atheneum, 2003) will know, one of the main reasons the Salem witch trials came to an end is that Increase Mather decided that "it were better that ten suspected witches should escape, than that one innocent person should be condemned," pp. 181–82. This was the exact opposite of what Shepard had argued. One might argue that the seventy-year passage from one view to the other is a key to understanding the history of the Puritan colony.

pp. 51–52 For Shepard, see MH, p. 71.

pp. 52–53 Unearthing Vane's role in these controversies is one of Winship's most important contributions. On Vane's background, see MH, p. 50. For Cyclone Covey's description of Vane, see PW, p. 91. For Winthrop's response to Cotton, see PD, p. 137.

pp. 52–53 Winship questions whether the Cotton-led revival ever took place; see MH p. 63 and 267, fn. 56.

p. 54 For Williams, Morgan's PD is again highly readable and well informed. The main focus of the work is Winthrop, and Morgan tends to see Williams from Winthrop's more moderate and inclusive point of view. A book written for general readers that concentrates on Williams himself is Edwin S. Gaustad, *Liberty of Conscience: Roger Williams in America* [hereafter LOC] (Grand Rapids, Mich.: Eerdmans, 1991). Gaustad is a noted historian of religion, and while the narrative is very similar to Morgan's, this more recent book includes some details and newer perspectives: for "middle walking" p. 25, "soul" and "act" p. 26. Historians have learned to their sorrow that a great deal of the original source material about Williams was lost in various disasters.

p. 56 For Bradford on Williams's views, see PD, p. 11. For Bradford on Williams's transition from belief to practice, see PD, p. 120.

pp. 57–58 For Williams on Indians and Europeans, and the poem, see LOC, pp. 28–29.

p. 58 For the quotation from Romans and the whole issue of Indians, the conversion of the Jews, and Puritan beliefs about America, see PO, p. 109. For Williams on the "sin" of taking the natives' land, see LOC, p. 32.

p. 58 For Williams on conversions, see LOC, p. 30.

p. 59 For Winthrop on there being enough land for all, see the quote in James Axtell, *The Invasion Within; The Contest of Cultures in Colonial North America* (New York: Oxford, 1985), p. 137. This book is required reading for anyone interested in studying the relationships between settlers and natives in the colonial period, but it is aimed at a college-level readership. I discuss Axtell in more detail below in a note to p. 75.

p. 61   For the Providence document, see LOC, p. 49.

CHAPTER FIVE: SPIRIT

p. 63   For the subhead phrase "The American Jezabel," see AC, p. 310. This section is Winthrop's account of the affair written shortly after it ended. Designed to be a proof that the community was right and Anne Hutchinson was wrong, it is of course biased but still worth reading. The eccentric spelling of "Jezabel" is Winthrop's.

p. 63   For Winthrop on Hutchinson, see AC, p. 263. This paragraph follows the interpretation Winship outlines in MH, p. 7.

p. 64   For Hutchinson on the Antichrist, see AC, pp. 336–37. This is taken from the record of her examination, which is not as obviously filtered as Winthrop's account but nonetheless has gaps. It was first published by one of her descendants, the loyalist Thomas Hutchinson, 130 years later. It would be simplistic to see either as a completely objective account of what took place during her trial. A better strategy is to read both, and to consult the commentaries of historians who have studied them and all the other surviving records.

pp. 64–66 A recent and well-received academic study of this period takes as its focus the problem that outspoken women posed to the Puritan leadership. See Jane Kamensky, *Governing the Tongue: The Politics of Speech in Early New England* (New York: Oxford, 1997). She urges caution in following the accounts in which Hutchinson claims to have had revelations from God, since that gave the elders a clear-cut ground on which to banish her, p. 80. This book is aimed at college-level readers and will be of most use to teachers and highly motivated readers.

p. 65   On the hint of Hutchinson knowing about female preachers, see AC, p. 380, n. 18. For Eleanor Davis, see David Hall, *Worlds of Wonder, Days of Judgment: Popular Religious Belief in Early New England* (New York: Knopf, 1989), pp. 96–97. Filled with fascinating examples such as this and written for a general audience, it is a book well worth the effort for high school readers curious about the period. It investigates how the Puritans juggled their interest in magic, astrology, and other folk beliefs with their strict Protestantism.

pp. 65–66 Winship points out the rarity of chairs in MH, p. 55. Winship does not believe the popular interpretation that Hutchinson's ideas appealed to merchants because of their business interests, and his comments are so assured and scathing that they have a slight edge of humor; see MH, p. 74 and fn. 33, p. 271. I have included the idea here because it is one students are sure to see in textbooks for a long time to come.

p. 67 For Wheelwright's fast-day sermon, see PD, p. 143.

p. 67 For Winthrop on "knit" in his "Model of Christian Charity," see PiA, p. 91.

p. 67 For the two meanings of "reduce" in this context, see PO, p. 138.

pp. 68–72 The trial quotations are from AC, pp. 312–48.

p. 69 For the accusation that Hutchinson preached a kind of familist free love, see AC, p. 363.

p. 71 The modern historian is Jane Kamensky; see the note above to p. 60.

p. 72 For a possible medical explanation for Hutchinson's "monstrous birth," see PO, p. 146.

p. 73 For Shepard's, views see Hall's introduction to AC, pp. 18–19.

CHAPTER SIX: WAR

p. 75 An older view that blamed the Pequot for being "savage" and justified the Puritans' acts has been debunked. A more modern view, which blames the Puritans for greed and their own savagery, is still upheld, especially by the expert on Indians in this period, Francis Jennings. Cave carefully considers many reasons for the Puritans' behavior in the war, including territorial greed, competition with other European settlers, and economic calculations, but in the end sees their beliefs as central. See his introduction to PW, pp. 1–10 for a good survey of these themes. Another thoughtful review of the older views of this war can be found in PO, p. 107.

p. 75 For the Pequot quotation, see James Axtell, *Natives and Newcomers: The Cultural Origins of North America* (New York: Oxford, 2001), p. 61. Axtell is one of the best-known experts on the Indians and the English in this period. He uses the tools of anthropology as well as history, and while not as much of a partisan as Jennings, he has done much to change historians' views. He writes well, but for a college-level audience.

p. 76   For Mason's commission, see PW, p. 137.

p. 77   For wampum and the role it may have played in the Pequot War, see PW, pp. 51–54.

p. 77   For Williams's sea journey, see LOC, p. 50.

p. 78   For Williams on the native view of killing women and children, see Karen Ordahl Kupperman, *Indians & English: Facing Off in Early America* [hereafter IE] (Ithaca, N.Y.: Cornell University Press, 2000), p. 230.

pp. 78–80 The view that the most completely destructive campaign is, in a way, the most humane since it brings the war to an end rapidly is still held today. The *New York Times Magazine* interviewed Lieutenant Colonel Bryan McCoy while the recent war in Iraq was taking place. He said, "There's no sense in trying to refine it, the crueler it is, the sooner it's over" (see "Good Kills," by Peter Maass, 4/20/03, p. 34).

p. 78   For "severe justice," see IE, p. 233.

p. 78   For the Pequot taunts, see PW, p. 136.

p. 79   For "too furious," see IE, p. 230.

p. 80   For Underhill's conscience pangs, see IE, p. 230.

p. 80   For Underhill on "terrible death," see PW, p. 152; for the conclusion that the Pequot War signaled a view that all natives should be destroyed, see PW, p. 173; for Williams adopting a Pequot boy, p. 159.

MEN ON HORSEBACK

CHAPTER SEVEN: "NO SMALL EVILS"

p. 83   For the chapter title and Laud quotation, see OCRP, p. 41. For "heathenish," see SAC, p. 118.

p. 86   For "English province," see SAC, p. 116.

p. 86   For the king's furious letter with its firm underlines, see Charles Carlton,

Charles I: The Personal Monarch [hereafter CCC] (London and New York: Routledge, 1983; 2nd ed., 1995), p. 206. This is one of the few modern biographies of Charles. Carlton's psychological interpretation of the king has been criticized by scholars, but it has much to offer. This is not the single biography a casual reader should read for pleasure or knowledge, but it is well worth consulting for insights into the king.

p. 86 For "just," see OCRP, p. 42; for the Scots proverb, see CCC, p. 204.

p. 87 For "army in Ireland," see OCRP, p. 44.

p. 88 For the subhead "I cannot," see CCC, p. x.

p. 89 For this portrait of the young Charles and its psychological view of his troubles see CCC, pp. 4–10. For Henry, see p. 10.

p. 91 For Charles's "word of a king," see Michael B. Young, *Charles I* [hereafter YC] (New York: St. Martin's, 1997), p. 141. This book and Peter Gaunt's *Oliver Cromwell* [hereafter GOC] (Oxford, England, and Cambridge, Mass.: Blackwell, 1996) are surveys of scholarship on these key figures written for college and graduate students. Always focused simultaneously on the conflicting interpretations of generations of historians and the historical subjects themselves, they are fascinating reads. I would not suggest beginning with either book, but they are very useful resources.

p. 93 For Marshall's sermon, see EB, pp. 88–89. Hill's book is filled with telling examples and quotations such as this.

p. 94 For "birds" and "legal," see CCC, p. 233. For Milton, see HB, p. 180.

CHAPTER EIGHT: "A REBELLION AGAINST US AND THE LAW"

p. 95 For the chapter title, see Charles in YC, p. 153.

p. 97 For Cromwell on his lack of plans, see GOC, p. 22. Gaunt is particularly good on the Cromwell legends and the two alternative views of him. Scrupulously fair, he credits the most negative views while in the end not accepting them.

pp. 97–98 For "by birth," see GOC, p. 29.

p. 99 Graham Swift, *Waterland* (New York: Poseidon, 1983), p. 13.

pp. 100–1 For Cromwell's conversion, see GOC, p. 37.

p. 101   The anecdote about Cromwell recommending Ralegh's *History* to his son is repeated in all the biographies and is based on a surviving letter, so it is clearly true. In her version of the story, Antonia Fraser also includes the relevant quotation from Ralegh's *History*. See her *Cromwell, Our Chief of Men* [hereafter COCM] (London: Weidenfeld, 1973; Methuen paperback, 1985), p. 307. Fraser is a famous biographer who carefully reads through primary and secondary sources and weaves them together into a readable, engaging narrative. As in this example, she provides a great deal of useful, significant information, which is especially helpful for those not already familiar with this history. Hers is the standard biography for adult general readers, and any motivated teenager will have no trouble reading it, though at 772 pages its length may be daunting. I would encourage such readers to compare her account to that of Gaunt or other scholars, who often push further in their analysis of sources and events.

p. 102   For "give Caesar," see AMT, p. 151.

p. 102   For "Whore of Babylon," see EB, p. 185.

pp. 102–3 For the origins of "Roundhead" and "Cavalier," including the Prynne quotation, see COCM, p. 86. For Suckling's poem and the notes on it, see SEP, p. 318.

p. 105   For Wharton's comments, see Bob Carruthers, *The English Civil Wars: 1642–1660* [hereafter ECW] (London: Cassell, 2000), p. 52. This colorful book is a war buff's treatment of the conflict and has useful maps, details, and quotations. It should be most appealing for the fan of military history. But the publisher also produces CD-ROMs and, like some of those involved in that field, seems to feel that permissions and credits are not necessary, which makes it difficult to trace his materials.

p. 108   For "triumphal entry," see Austin Woolrych, *Battles of the English Civil War: Marston Moor, Naseby, Preston* [hereafter BECW] (New York: Macmillan, 1961; paperback ed. London: Phoenix, 2000), p. 13. This is a vivid, clear, knowledgeable account by the expert in this field. It has much to offer those interested in military history. Anyone who enjoys reading accounts of the battles of the American Civil War will get a great deal out of this book.

p. 108   For "Come, my boys," see BECW, p. 17.

p. 110   For Charles on York, see BECW, p. 57.

Chapter Nine: Marston Moor

pp. 111–12 For "forlorn hope," see BECW, p. 67. My account of the battle of Marston Moor draws heavily on both Woolrych and Carruthers, and I strongly urge anyone interested in this fascinating battle to read Woolrych's engagingly written and consummately professional account, and to consult the clear and colorful guide to troop movements in Carruthers.

p. 113 For "We will charge" and this vivid account of the weather, see BECW, p. 71.

p. 114 The often-repeated quotation about the sound and smoke of the battle can be found on many websites devoted to the English Civil War—for example, www.thevickerage.worldonline.co.uk/ecivil/marston_moor.htm. This is an informative and well-illustrated site that will be of especial interest to military history buffs who enjoy mapping out each moment of a battle. For "we came down the hill," see BECW, pp. 71–72.

p. 116 For "in the fire" and "wae," see BECW, p. 75. For the colors of the various troops, see COCM, p. 123.

p. 119 For Cromwell's famous line about "plain russet-coated captain," see GOC, p. 49. For Manchester's dislike of these troops, see GOC, p. 50. For Denzil Holles on the tradesmen as colonels, see BECW, p. 103. He was talking about the New Model Army, not just Cromwell's forces, although Cromwell was influential in forming that national force, as I describe below.

p. 120 For Cromwell on "sober," see GOC, p. 51; on "the state," p. 55.

p. 120 For Cromwell's letter to the Scots, see Lesley LeClaire, "The Survival of the Manuscript," in Michael Mendle, ed., *The Putney Debates of 1647: The Army, the Levellers and the English State* [hereafter TPD] (Cambridge, England: Cambridge, 2001), p. 29. This is a collection of academic essays that requires a basic knowledge of the history of the English Civil War, and especially the Putney Debates, which I discuss in chapter eleven. Like so many high-level works, it contains gems not found in secondary material; it would be of most interest to the teacher or student doing a lengthy thesis or report.

p. 120 On "liberty," see GOC, p. 58.

p. 120   For Manchester on visions, see GOC, p. 50. For Winthrop on "liberty of conscience," see PD, p. 183.

Chapter Ten: The New Model

p. 123   For Cromwell's supposed desire to rid England of the nobility, see GOC, p. 59.

p. 123   I am especially grateful to Dr. Bremer for reminding me of the distinction between the kind of religious toleration Cromwell favored and the more modern view in which we do not assume any faith is more true than another and believe letting all beliefs flourish is a good in itself. In writing this paragraph I have borrowed some of the language of his note to me clarifying this distinction.

pp. 123–24 For Cromwell on his men and the Self-Denying Ordinance, see BECW, p. 91.

pp. 125–26 For Leicester, see ECW, p. 167; the comments are from a contemporary diary.

p. 128   For Cromwell on his confidence before the battle of Naseby, see BECW, pp. 125–26.

p. 130   For Cromwell's letters from the battlefield, see BECW, p. 136.

p. 131   For Marshall on God's curse for cowards, see PO, p. 102.

p. 131   For Cotton, see PiA, p. 109.

p. 132   For "deadly fasting," see PE, pp. 124–25.

Heaven or Hell?

Chapter Eleven: Agreement of the People

p. 137   For the subhead, see COCM, p. 212. For "every man," see Colonel Thomas Rainborough in Joseph Bergin, ed., *The Short Oxford History of Europe: The Seventeenth Century* (Oxford, England: Oxford, 2001), p. 78.

p. 139   For James Pitson, see LeClaire in TPD, p. 29. For Cromwell on "authority," see COCM, p. 191.

p. 140   For "Golden Ball," see COCM, p. 192.

p. 140   For "mercenary army," see AMT, p. 175.

p. 141   For the king's exclamation "you cannot," see COCM, p. 204.

p. 142   I found many interesting and useful resources about Lilburne, the Levellers, and the Putney Debates online. Skyhook is, again, an excellent starting place. For Lilburne's revelation, see D. B. Robertson, *The Religious Foundations of Leveller Democracy* [hereafter RF] (New York: King's Crown, 1951), p. 14. I actually read this online, too, via Questia, a subscription-based service that gives readers easy access to a wealth of books. The search functions are very helpful, and you can quickly browse through many sources. The only problem is that Questia's collection is mainly made up of out-of-print older books, which must be used with caution, or very recent academic studies, which will be tough going for high school readers. The best bet would be to use it as a supplementary resource to find additional information about people and topics. Start either in a regular library, with a librarian's help, or by consulting the *Columbia Encyclopedia* on Questia; otherwise, you will have many references but little chance of making sense of them.

p. 143   For Milton on majority and minority, see AMT, p. 190. For Lilly, see note to p. 112.

p. 143   For the subhead "The Poorest He," see AMT, p. 176.

p. 143   Copies of the "Agreement" are easily available on the Internet. I found the annotated version at www.strecorsoc.org particularly useful. This site has a Quaker point of view and is explicitly favorable to the Levellers and, in general, to what it considers to be the politics of activism for the people. Following links from Skyhook will also lead you to the "Agreement," as well as transcripts of the Putney Debates. A useful reference site with many documents, including the "Agreement," is Constitutional Documents of the Puritan Revolution at www.constitution.org/eng/conpur.htm.

pp. 144–46 For Cromwell's cautions about imposing new ideas on people, see Austin Woolrych, "The Debates from the Perspective of the Army," in TPD, p. 69.

p. 147   For Lilburne, see RF, p. 11. Historians are not sure whether Hale said the famous line at all, but if he did, or even if it was attributed to him, it was probably a quotation from a 1713 play called *Cato*. I have not yet been able to determine if the play was quoting Lilburne, though given the politics of Joseph Addison, its author, that is possible. For Ireton and Sexby, as well as Rainborough's famous response, and the subhead on p. 117, see LeClaire in TPD, p. 32.

p. 148   For Wildman's unmistakable anticipation of the principles of American democracy, see George L. Abernethy, ed., *The Idea of Equality: An Anthology* (Richmond, Va: Knox, 1959), p. 110. This is a compilation of primary sources from throughout western history, and it has a chapter featuring Lilburne's work. I also found this book on Questia.

p. 149   For John Lilburne on women, see HB, p. 185. For the dismissive response to the women's petition, see Patricia Crawford, "The Poorest She," in TPD, p. 210.

p. 150   For Katherine Chidley, see HB, pp. 185–86, and Crawford in TPD, p. 210.

CHAPTER TWELVE: THE INNER LIGHT

p. 151   For the subhead, see COCM, p. 291.

p. 152   For Cromwell on the hand of God, see GOC, p. 96. For "draw down," see EB, p. 326.

p. 153   For Lovelace, see his "To Lucasta. From Prison," in SEP, p. 359.

p. 153   Peter Gaunt quotes a letter of Cromwell's with the Phinehas analogy in GOC on p. 105.

p. 155   For Charles's behavior and the executioner's line, see note for p. 123. For the possible link between the Levellers and later developments in England, see Tim Harris, "The Leveller Legacy," in TPD, pp. 237–38.

pp. 155–56 For Winstanley, see EB, p. 126, p. 134.

p. 157   For "stinking vapor," see Christine Leigh Heyrman, *Commerce and Culture: The Maritime Communities of Colonial Massachusetts, 1690–1750* (New York: Norton, 1984), p. 109. Though an academic book, this is an excellent and readable account. I touch on Quakers and accusations of witchcraft in my *Witch-Hunt*.

pp. 159–60 This account of Cromwell in Ireland, including the new sense of whom he fought at Drogheda, is from HB, pp. 205–12. A similarly balanced reading of the battles, putting the slaughter in the context of warfare at the time, can be found in

GOC, pp. 116–20. Both are clearly written in response to earlier and more damning accounts in which Cromwell is portrayed as a monster. Those views are still current in Ireland, and among some Irish Americans, today.

pp. 160–61 For Cromwell and the Parliament of Saints, see GOC, "called by God," p. 147, "judgment by love," p. 149.

EPILOGUE: BRITISH HELL, AMERICAN PROMISE

p. 168   For Milton, see John Milton, *Paradise Lost,* Merritt Y. Hughes, ed. (New York: Odyssey, Bobbs-Merrill, 1962); "Hail" and the famous passage on reigning are on p. 13.

p. 170   For the 1776 revival, see Rhys Isaac, *The Transformation of Virginia, 1740–1790* (Chapel Hill, N.C.: University of North Carolina Press, 1982), p. 261. This Pulitzer Prize–winning history is a treat for anyone curious not only about American history but about novel ways in which it can be researched and described.

p. 171   I found this transcription of lines from Dr. King's much-quoted last speech on the Internet by searching under "Martin Luther King last speech," which led me to The Martin Luther King Jr. Papers Project, www.stanford.edu/group/King/sitemap.htm, where you can find a complete transcript of the speech, including crowd reactions.

p. 171   For Waller, see SEP, p. 295.

TIMELINE

YEAR	ENGLAND, SCOTLAND, IRELAND
1600	Charles, son of King James VI of Scotland, born East India Company founded
1603	James becomes James I, king of England and Scotland
1604	James meets Puritan leaders and does not agree with their views of religion
1607	
1608	Sir Walter Ralegh imprisoned, becomes tutor to James's heir, Henry
1611	King James translation of the Bible published
1612	Henry, eldest son of James, dies
1613	Sir Walter Ralegh's *History of the World* published
1618	Ralegh executed on charge of treason
1619	
1620	
1625	James dies; Charles becomes king Charles marries Henrietta Maria; aids Catholics in France; Parliament objects
1626	
1628	Led by John Pym, Parliament insists that the king cannot levy taxes it has not agreed to William Laud made Bishop of London
1629	Charles dissolves Parliament
1630	Charles signs peace treaty with Catholic Spain John Cotton speaks to departing Puritans
1631	
1633	*The British Heaven* performed for Charles I William Laud appointed Archbishop of Canterbury, highest post in the Church of England Led by Thomas Wentworth, Lord Strafford, English take Irish land to establish new plantations Charles crowned king of Scotland
1634	Ship money revived William Prynne publishes *Histrio-Mastix*, tried, convicted, punished

THE NEW WORLD	EUROPE, ASIA, INDIA
Jamestown Settlement	
	Thirty Years' War between Catholics and Protestants begins
First African slaves in Jamestown	
Plymouth Colony	Major defeat for Protestants near Prague
First English settlement at Salem	
John Winthrop agrees to lead group to Massachusetts	
Arbella crosses Atlantic	
Winthrop writes "A Model of Christian Charity"	
Roger Williams comes to Massachusetts	
All free, male church members in Massachusetts allowed to vote	
Cotton immigrates to Massachusetts	Galileo forced to recant
Anne and William Hutchinson arrive in Boston	

YEAR	ENGLAND, SCOTLAND, IRELAND
1635	Ship money extended to whole country
1636	Charles collects ship money again
1637	John Hampden loses ship money case Scots protest English prayer book
1638	Scots sign National Covenant against Charles's church reforms
1639	Charles prepares to attack Scotland; Scots gather troops
1640	Charles calls Parliament to finance war, Parliament demands reforms, Charles dismisses Parliament; Scots invade England; Charles calls Parliament again; legislators insist on trying Laud and Wentworth
1641	House of Commons approves forces to destroy images in churches; Wentworth tried and executed; rebellion in Ireland; Parliament delivers Grand Remonstrance
1642	Charles gathers forces, begins English Civil War; battles of Edgehill and Turnham Green
1643	Hampden killed; Prince Rupert takes city of Bristol; Parliament agrees to Solemn League and Covenant; Charles bring men from Ireland
1644	Scotland enters war on Parliament's side July 2, battle of Marston Moor: Oliver Cromwell leads Parliament to victory Self-Denying Ordinance bars members of Parliament from leading army
1645	Laud executed Cromwell made Lieutenant General; army reorganized as New Model Army under command of Sir Thomas Fairfax Marquis of Montrose leads Royalists to series of victories in Scotland May–July, battle of Naseby: Cromwell and New Model Army defeat Charles and Rupert
1646	Charles surrenders to Scots
1647	Parliament pays £400,000 and gains control of king; Charles taken by George Joyce; king escapes to Isle of Wight George Fox begins to preach Putney Debates: Levellers argue for new government in which many free men can vote
1648	Charles sides with Scots, who invade England; Cromwell enters Scotland and wins battle of Preston Thomas Pride purges Parliament
1649	Charles beheaded; Cromwell lands in Ireland, destroys Drogheda and Wexford Gerrard Winstanley publishes Digger Manifesto
1651	Cromwell defeats forces led by Charles, son of executed king; Charles escapes to France

THE NEW WORLD	EUROPE, ASIA, INDIA
Roger Williams banished Anne Hutchinson hosts gatherings to discuss Cotton's sermons Henry Vane Jr. elected governor of Massachussets Colony Warned by Winthrop, Williams escapes Boston, settles in Providence Pequot War begins	
Anne Hutchinson tried, banished Puritans massacre Pequots, including women and children Defeated by Winthrop in new election, Vane returns to England	
	East India company begins building city of Madras
	Louis XIV becomes King of France
New England Way defined, Congregationalist church order adopted	Treaty of Westphalia ends Thirty Years' War; greater toleration for variety of Christian beliefs is one provision
John Winthrop dies	

YEAR	ENGLAND, SCOTLAND, IRELAND
1653	Cromwell supervises selection of new Parliament but is frustrated with its actions; is named Lord Protector
1656	
1658	Cromwell dies; son Richard named Lord Protector
1659	Army favoring Charles gathers in Scotland
1660	Leaders of Protectorate's army decide not to fight against Charles's men; Charles becomes King Charles II
1661	Charles II forbids execution of Quakers
1662	Vane executed on charges of having helped to bring about the death of Charles I
1664-66	Isaac Newton develops his law of gravitation
1667	*Paradise Lost* published
1672	James, son of Charles II, is received into the Roman Catholic Church
1685	Charles II dies; his son reigns as James II
1686	
1687	Isacc Newton publishes Mathematical Principals of Natural Philosophy, including his laws of motion
1689	William and Mary, both Protestants, agree to new kind of rule in combination with Parliament Parliament passes Toleration Act, freedom of worship for all brands of Protestants in England and colonies
1690	
1692	
1740	
1757	
1776	

Note: Puritan dates in the timeline are based on a similar and more extensive chronology in Bremer, *Puritan Experiment*.

THE NEW WORLD	EUROPE, ASIA, INDIA
Quakers banished from Massachusetts	
Death penalty for Quakers who return to Massachusetts	
	Bombay given to England as part of queen's dowry
	Calculus invented independently by Newton and G. W. Leibnitz
	Treaty of Breda, English give up Suriname to Dutch, retain New York
Sir Edmund Andros appointed governor of New England	
Andros overthrown	
	City of Calcutta founded by East India Company
19 convicted witches hanged in Salem	
George Whitefield stimulates Great Awakening	
	English defeat ruler of Bengal, now dominant power in richest region of India
Mixed congregations of black and white Christians	

Index

Note: Page numbers in *italic type* refer to illustrations.